Facilitation Techniques for Consultants

Indispensable tools to engage clients, improve meetings and build collaborative teams

Ingrid Bens, M.Ed.
Certified Professional Facilitator

FACILITATION TECHNIQUES FOR CONSULTANTS

INGRID BENS
Published by FACILITATION TUTOR LLC

ISBN: 978-0-9970970-0-9
LCCN: 2015920411

Table of Contents

Introduction

Every consultant needs to know how to facilitate, even expert consultants who make their living giving advice. There are two reasons for this.

First, there's the fact that being a consultant involves running lots of meetings: meetings to set parameters, clarify needs, identify outcomes, uncover risks, agree on roles, coordinate schedules, assess progress and solve problems. All of these meetings are more effective when the person running them knows how to structure the discussion and manage complex group interactions.

The second reason is that facilitation tools and techniques are useful for managing the inevitable ups and downs that are part of every project. That's because facilitators have developed techniques for proactively finding and solving problems.

Since the education of most professional consultants is focused on technical mastery, facilitation training is usually skipped. This is a major oversight, considering just how much time consultants spend working with groups. This book aims to bridge that knowledge gap by describing the essential facilitation techniques that every consultant needs to know.

This book is not a manual on consulting skills. It doesn't give advice on marketing, managing the consultant-client relationship, writing effective contracts, navigating organizational politics or any of the other topics usually covered in books about consulting. Instead, this book is about the specific facilitation tools that will help every expert consultant become even more effective.

Two Types of Consulting

In order to provide some context, let's briefly explore how the practice of facilitation fits into the world of the expert consultant.

When most people hear the word *consultant,* they immediately assume that it refers to someone who's paid to give advice. This impression is generally correct, since that's what most professional consultants are paid to do. There is, however, a whole other type of consulting in which no advice is given at all. This is known as *Process Consulting.*

Process Consultation involves assessing the client situation in order to identify the strategies clients can use to improve their situation for themselves. *Process Consultants* don't offer advice. Instead, they <u>facilitate</u> a series of structured dialogues in order to help their clients arrive at their own solutions and action plans. Instead of being paid for their advice, *Process Consultants* are paid for the work they do as facilitators.

Facilitation Techniques for Consultants

Expert consultants typically come from fields like accounting, engineering and architecture. They help clients with technically challenging initiatives such as designing buildings, implementing new technology, overhauling accounting systems and realigning organizational structures. During these initiatives, expert consultants work as advisors, designers and sometimes even as the hands-on managers of the change initiative. <u>Expert consultants are paid to tell the client what to do.</u>

Process consultants typically come from fields like adult education, industrial psychology and other applied behavioral sciences. They're skilled at team building, conflict mediation and improving organizational culture. They do things like facilitate planning sessions, conduct feedback meetings and lead structured problem-solving sessions. <u>Process consultants are paid to ask the right questions so that clients can identify the way forward for themselves.</u>

At first glance, it looks like these two types of consulting are mutually exclusive. In fact, nothing could be further from the truth! It turns out that all expert consultants need to be able to act like *Process Consultants* at strategically selected moments during every consulting assignment. In other words, there are times when it's better to ask questions and listen to the client, than it is to be directive and tell the client what to do.

Expert consultants help their clients by sharing their knowledge. They:
<ul><li>study the client situation</li><li>determine what their clients need</li><li>provide advice about what their clients should do in the form of a report, set of drawings and ongoing coaching</li><li>sometimes act as the hands-on manager of the change initiative</li></ul>

Process consultants help their clients by <u>facilitating</u> them through structured conversations that enable the clients to make critical decisions for themselves. They:
<ul><li>involve clients in assessment activities so that they can better understand client needs, resources, opportunities, blocks and barriers</li><li>facilitate a variety of structured dialogues so that clients can define the parameters of the change they seek</li><li>help clients identify blocks to progress and systematically remove them</li><li>help clients settle disputes and overcome barriers to change</li><li>help clients set goals and develop plans to implement them</li><li>encourage clients to create mechanisms that keep the change on track</li></ul>

Using Both Consulting Styles

Right now, most expert consultants know how to conduct the activities listed in the column on the left side in the chart below. The message of this book is that all expert consultants would be more effective if they also knew how to conduct the activities listed in the column on the right.

Typical Expert Consulting Activities...	Typical Process Consultation Activities...

- Doing research
- Advocating a course of action in writing
- Providing expertise
- Providing training
- Advising as action unfolds
- Coaching clients
- Directing activities
- Monitoring results
- Evaluating activities
- Writing a final report
	- Facilitating clients while they:
	  - assess the situation
	  - identify internal resources
	  - clarify their goals for the project
	  - set benchmarks
	  - assess risks and barriers
	
	- Facilitating clients while they:
	  - develop implementation strategies
	  - clarify their roles and responsibilities
	
	- Facilitating feedback activities like:
	  - customer satisfaction surveys
	  - midpoint checks
	  - after-action reviews
	
	- Facilitating problem-solving and trouble-shooting sessions
	
	- Facilitating conflict-mediation activities
	
	- Helping clients evaluate outcomes

When to Use Facilitation

The question of when to use facilitation has a really simple answer: facilitating is the right approach to use whenever it's more important to hear from clients than it is to tell them what to do.

Some examples of times to switch into the facilitation role include when:

- gathering information in order to build a client profile
- assessing the environmental factors affecting a project
- clarifying goals and agreeing on benchmarks
- agreeing on roles and responsibilities
- identifying risks and risk-mitigation strategies
- building client commitment and buy-in
- assessing progress
- identifying and solving problems
- settling disputes
- overcoming resistance to change
- evaluating outcomes

Expert consultants gain real benefit from strategically using facilitation during consulting assignments, because facilitation ensures that:

- the voice of the client is heard
- the client is engaged at every stage
- the client buys into major decisions
- the talents and resources of the client group are fully leveraged
- the client takes responsibility for their actions
- there's a mechanism to surface issues and resolve them
- the client is fully committed to implementing change

In addition, becoming a skilled facilitator helps to ensure that every meeting is more efficient — something that will benefit every project!

Content Overview

This book is divided into two sections. In the first chapter of Part One, there's an overview of the core practices of facilitation. Chapter Two explores the importance of questioning and offers insights about when and how to use different question types. This is followed by a chapter that describes the main techniques used to help groups make decisions. Chapter Four offers specific strategies for both preventing and resolving conflict. Part One ends with a chapter that contains practical suggestions about how to make any meeting more productive and engaging.

Part Two of this book describes the essential conversations that every expert consultant needs to be able to facilitate. These dialogues are laid out in clear, step-by-step detail so that they're easy to apply. These discussions translate the concept of facilitation into practical activities.

This book is short on theory, but long on application. Instead of wordy pages of dense text, it leans toward offering only essential information. Wherever possible, ideas and tools are provided as bullet points and at-a-glance summaries.

Since we live in the digital age, more and more business meetings are conducted using the Internet or through conference calls. While the information in this book is primarily described in terms of face-to-face meetings, the structured dialogues in this book are described as both face-to-face meetings and as virtual meetings.

I'm confident that you'll find *Facilitation Techniques for Consultants* to be both practical and indispensable!

Ingrid Bens, M.Ed.,
Certified Professional Facilitator

Definitions

Consultant
An outsider who is asked to help change or improve a situation, process or structure over which he or she has no direct control.

Client
The person, group or organization seeking to either solve a problem or create an opportunity. The client owns and controls the entity that's being improved.

Intervention
Any action taken to improve the effectiveness of a group or a system. Making a positive intervention is the goal of all consulting activities.

Consultation
A two-way interaction: a process of seeking, giving and receiving help. Consulting is aimed at helping a person, group or organization identify opportunities, deal with problems, optimize internal resources and make positive change.

Expert Consulting
This involves assessing the client situation in order to determine an effective course of action and then offering expertise. Expert consultants are paid to tell clients what to do. Expert consultants typically provide written recommendations. In some cases, they also directly manage specific project components. Examples of expert consulting includes architects who design new buildings, engineers who oversee construction projects, IT specialists who advise on systems upgrades, accountants who install new accounting systems, and management consultants who help large organizations overhaul their internal structure.

Process Consulting
This involves helping clients assess their own situation, then offering specific processes so that clients can develop and implement their own strategies for change. Process consultants do not tell clients what to do. Instead, they facilitate a series of structured conversations that enable clients to make their own decisions about the best way forward. They help clients identify and mobilize their own resources. Examples of Process Consultation activities include team-building activities, strategic-planning retreats, process-improvement initiatives, conflict-mediation sessions and change-implementation efforts.

Facilitation
This is an approach to group management that's based on asking instead of telling. Facilitators give meetings an orderly structure and then keep discussions focused to ensure that a constructive outcome is achieved. Facilitators deliberately stay out of the conversation to ensure that the clients are making their own decisions. Facilitators help clients identify the goals that are meaningful to them and engage them as active participants in achieving their desired outcomes.

Open Space
A self-organizing meeting held in a very large room with thirty or more participants. A broad, open description of the meeting purpose is posted. Participants sit in chairs arranged in a circle. A list of issues and opportunities related to the purpose is generated by the participants. People then break themselves into small groups around these issues and opportunities. Small groups explore topics for a period of time. Participants are then invited to stay with that topic or move freely between groups to continue the exploration, learning and problem solving. A plenary is held at the end of the meeting to bring ideas back to the larger forum. This approach is notable for its initial lack of an agenda and trust in the participants' ability to identify the topics that need to be the focus of exploration. A distinguished proponent of this approach is NASA.

World Café
A more structured form of *Open Space* dialogue. A large group of participants circulate between a series of tables where they discuss a pre-determined topic and answer a set of pre-planned questions. Group movement is timed and everyone eventually visits each discussion topic. A café ambience is created in order to facilitate conversation. As well as speaking and listening, individuals are encouraged to write or doodle on paper tablecloths so that when people change tables they can see what previous members have expressed in their own words and images. The first *World Café* event was organized in 1995, and since then, the number of people who have participated in these events is estimated to be in the tens of thousands.

Work Out
A discussion method pioneered at General Electric in the 1980's and is still in use today. *Work Out* is a one-day, and sometimes two-day, problem-solving event that brings together cross-functional staff teams, customers and suppliers to identify problems occurring within a process, product or service. Participants meet in small groups to identify problems, analyze them in depth and identify actionable solutions. At the end of a *Work Out*, a Town Hall meeting is held to share recommendations with the total group. Five to ten executives are on hand at these Town Hall sessions to comment on the proposals, give on-the-spot approval and commit to serve as champions for staff actions.

Chapter One - Facilitation 101

Let's start with a definition:

> **A facilitator** is someone who helps a group of people clarify their needs, identify their common goals, make joint decisions and create action plans to achieve the outcomes that are important to them.

Facilitation was created to ensure that the voice of group members is heard. In order to leverage their talents and gain their commitment, facilitators always stay out of the discussion. This frees them up to focus on the process or how the conversation is structured and managed. This includes such things as defining the order in which topics will be discussed, the questions that will be asked and the specific decision-making tools that will be used.

Another way of understanding the role is to think of facilitators as referees. In that role they:

- provide an orderly sequence of activities

- watch the action, more than participate in it

- ensure that group members have effective rules to guide interaction

- keep discussion focused

- keep their finger on the pulse so they know when to move on or wrap up

- help group members achieve closure and identify next steps

Facilitation is a Mindset

When you step into the facilitator role, you're making a commitment to act according to a specific set of beliefs: All facilitators firmly believe that:

- People are intelligent, capable and want to do the right thing.
- It's important to ensure that all voices are heard.
- Everyone's ideas can add value.
- Groups can often make a better decision than one person can make alone.
- People are more committed to the ideas and plans that they have helped to create.

Any time you adopt these beliefs and practice the techniques of facilitation, you're implicitly making a commitment to engage in dialogue, really listen and make decisions collaboratively.

The Importance of Staying Neutral

Facilitation was designed to be a neutral role so that the voices of group members are heard. Facilitators maintain neutrality simply by asking questions instead of making statements.

As an expert consultant, you may be wondering whether or not you really need to stay neutral when leading discussions with your clients. If you find yourself questioning this notion, you're not alone. Staying neutral doesn't come naturally to anyone and may actually seem like the wrong strategy to use when people are paying you to give them advice.

Despite the fact that neutrality may seem counterintuitive, there are some really good reasons to stay neutral during pre-selected conversations:

1. You're not going to be facilitating all the time; you're just going to use it for those conversations when it's really important to gather input.

2. Once you've declared that you want to hear from them, clients will expect you to listen to and accommodate their ideas. If you announce that you want to hear their ideas but then constantly interject your opinions, clients may stop sharing their thoughts. This is especially true if you contradict them.

3. Slipping into and out of the neutral role to chip in your ideas can make your efforts at facilitation look manipulative: on the one hand you say you want to hear from them, but then you constantly say things to influence group member thinking.

4. Staying neutral doesn't mean that you have to withhold good ideas or that you shouldn't help clients if they get stuck. That's because staying neutral has parameters that enable you to provide guidance without losing your neutrality. These parameters are described on the next page.

5. Most conflicts simply can't be managed unless you stay above the fray.

The Parameters of Neutrality

One of the most pervasive misconceptions about staying neutral is that it means totally withholding your expertise. Instead, staying neutral actually means avoiding contradicting, overruling or influencing the thinking of the client. That leaves you lots of room to use your technical expertise to ask the right probing questions and to offer helpful suggestions for the client to consider. The bottom line is that you can add your ideas into the mix as long as you do it in such a way that clients don't feel they've lost the right to decide. Use the following strategies to offer expertise while still preserving your neutrality.

1st Strategy—Ask Questions

If you have an idea that can help the group, or if you think that the group is overlooking an important idea, you don't have to bite your lip. Instead, introduce your idea in the form a question that sparks deeper thought.

> **Example:** If the group is spinning its wheels because they can't afford new computers, the facilitator is still neutral even if she asks: *"What are the benefits of renting new computers as an interim strategy?"*

Neutrality is preserved because the questioning merely prompts the group to consider another option, but doesn't tell them whether or not to pursue that idea.

2nd Strategy—Offer Suggestions

Another way to share a good idea while neutral is to offer the group a suggestion for their consideration. The key is to ensure that your tone of voice sounds like you're just putting something on the table for them to think about.

> **Example:** *"Why don't you take a few minutes to discuss the potential of outsourcing the IT function during the reorganization process. Let's look at the pros and cons so you can make an informed decision."*

Facilitator neutrality is preserved, because the final decision-making power remains with the group, despite the fact that the facilitator offered a new alternative to consider.

3rd Strategy—Take Off the Facilitator's Hat

If you're with a group that's about to make a serious mistake, and all of the questioning and suggesting in the world hasn't moved them in the right direction, facilitators sometimes step out of the neutral role to share information that's important.

In these rare cases, it's important for facilitators to clearly indicate that they're stepping out of the facilitator role:

> **Example:** *"I need to step out of the role of facilitator for a minute to tell you that the office location you're considering is not close to any of the rapid transit corridors approved for development during the next twenty years."*

Taking off the facilitator hat is only done when questioning and suggesting have not worked and when you have important information that the group needs to know. Be warned that leaping in and out of the neutral role too often sends the message to group members that their ideas could be overturned at any time.

Learn to say *"Okay"*

- When group members bring up what seems like an excellent point, facilitators can be tempted to congratulate that person by saying *"Good point"* or *"Great idea."* Unfortunately, this is a sure way to lose your neutrality, since it makes it look like you're agreeing and trying to influence the opinions of the group. To avoid this common pitfall, substitute *"Okay"* for *"Good point."*
- *Using "Okay"* enables you to acknowledge that you've heard a point, but doesn't indicate any approval on your part.
- In that same vein, whenever you're tempted to say, *"I like that idea,"* substitute *"Do the rest of you like that idea?"* After all, facilitators don't judge group member suggestions, but help them make those assessments themselves.

Introducing Facilitation to Clients

If you're working with a client group whose members are unfamiliar with the concept, it's a good idea to consider doing the following before stepping into the role:

1. Announce to the client that you're planning to be neutral during a specific discussion.

2. Explain why you won't be adding your ideas.

3. Describe what you will be doing during the facilitated dialogue.

4. Post a sheet of flip-chart paper on a side wall and explain that you'll be using it to park any issues or questions that members may ask you during the facilitation session, for a later response.

Even when you do all this, don't be surprised if your clients nonetheless ask for your opinion. Be aware that anytime you cave in to answer a direct question, you've stepped out of the facilitator role, and that losing neutrality works to undermine the purpose of structured discussions.

Balancing Facilitating With Giving Advice

In an ideal world you would have easy access to a skilled facilitator anytime you wanted to hold a meeting. Unfortunately, neutral facilitators are rarely available, which means that you'll usually have to play both roles. While this isn't ideal, it can be done. Here are some strategies:

- Act as the non-neutral chairperson for the overall meeting.
- Identify those agenda items where you'll be making a presentation, giving an update or sharing your expertise. You will not be facilitating those sessions.
- Identify those agenda items where you need to hear from the client. This is when you will be using your neutral facilitation skills.
- Explain to the client that you'll be more interested in listening than offering expertise during those sessions. Then stick to being neutral during those agenda items to ensure that the client is heard.

Facilitator Language

Facilitators have developed a distinct way of speaking. This language was created to make it possible to comment on people's behavior without sounding critical or judgmental. Here are the four most important language techniques:

1. Paraphrasing involves describing, in your own words, what another person's remarks convey.

> *"So you're saying. . ."*
> *"I'm picking up that you think. . ."*
> *"What I'm hearing you say is . . ."*

Facilitators paraphrase continuously, especially if the discussion starts to spin in circles, or if the conversation becomes heated. This repetition assures participants that their ideas are being heard. New facilitators often make the mistake of not paraphrasing enough.

2. Reporting behavior which consists of stating the specific, observable actions of others without making accusations or generalizations about them as people or attributing motives to them.

> *"I'm noticing that we've only heard from three people throughout most of this discussion."*
> *"I'm noticing that several people are looking at their email."*

By describing specific behaviors, facilitators give participants information about how their actions are being perceived. Feeding this information back to participants in a nonthreatening manner opens the door for individuals to suggest actions to improve the existing situation.

3. Descriptions of feelings which consist of specifying or identifying feelings by naming the feeling, or using a metaphor or a figure of speech.

> *"I feel frustrated. Is anyone else feeling that?"* (naming)
> *"I feel as if we're spinning our wheels."* (metaphor)
> *"I feel like we've hit the wall."* (figure of speech)

Facilitators always need to be in touch with how they're feeling and should not be afraid to share those feelings with the group. This grants others permission to also express feelings.

4. Perception checking which is describing another person's inner state in order to then check if that perception is correct.

> *"You appear upset by the last comment that was made. Are you?"*
> *"You seem impatient to move on to the next topic? Am I right?"*
> *"I see some frustration on your face. Am I reading you right?"*

Perception checking is a very important tool. It lets the facilitator take the pulse of participants without making incorrect assumptions.

Facilitation Core Practices

The first step in becoming a skilled facilitator is to understand that whenever you step into the role, you will need to employ certain core practices. No matter what the context or the other tools being used, facilitating means that you will always be doing the following ten things:

1. Stay neutral on the content.

The whole purpose of facilitating is to hear from the client, so staying out of the conversation is the hallmark of the facilitator role. Instead of trying to influence what the client thinks, the facilitator stays focused on providing structure and helping people have a productive conversation. When facilitators ask questions or offer helpful alternatives to consider, they never do this to impose their views or negate what the client wants.

2. Listen actively.

Since facilitating is all about getting the client to talk, listening is key. Active listening is listening to understand more than to judge. It also means using attentive body language and looking participants in the eye while they're speaking.

3. Ask questions.

Since facilitation is asking instead of telling, questioning is the most fundamental facilitator tool. Questions can be used to clarify ideas, probe for hidden information, challenge assumptions or ratify a consensus. Effective questioning encourages people to look past symptoms to get at root causes. The next chapter in this book offers tips about when and how to use questions effectively.

4. Paraphrase continuously.

The only real proof that you've actually heard what someone has said is to be able to accurately repeat their comments. For this reason, facilitators paraphrase continuously during discussions. Paraphrasing involves repeating what group members say. This lets people know that they were heard and acknowledges their input. Paraphrasing also lets others hear points for a second time.

5. Summarize discussions.

Facilitators summarize the ideas shared by members at the end of every discussion. They do this to ensure that everyone has heard all of the ideas that were shared, to check for accuracy, and to bring closure. Facilitators also summarize in the middle of discussions to catch everyone up on the conversation. Summarizing can also be useful to restart a stalled discussion. In these instances, summarizing reminds people of the points already discussed, which then sparks new thinking.

6. Record ideas.

Groups need to leave meetings with complete and accurate notes that summarize discussions. Facilitators do this on flip charts or on electronic whiteboards rather than on notepaper. This lets people see that their ideas are being recorded and helps focus the conversation.

7. Synthesize ideas.

Facilitators bounce ideas around the group to ensure that people build on each other's views. In non-decision-making conversations, they do this to build conversation and create synergy. In decision-making conversations, they ping-pong ideas around to ensure that each person's thoughts have been factored in. Once everyone has added their comments, the facilitator is able to make a statement that represents the views of the whole group.

8. Keep discussions on track.

If discussions veer off track or lose focus, facilitators notice this and tactfully point it out. They place a *Parking Lot* sheet on a wall and offer participants the option of "parking" extraneous topics for later discussion.

9. Test assumptions.

At the start of every discussion, facilitators outline the parameters of that topic, such as who is empowered to make which decisions, and any other constraints that might apply. This ensures that everyone is on the same page. They're always on the lookout for situations in which misunderstandings are rooted in differing assumptions, and they probe carefully to uncover these. They routinely invite people to clarify exactly what they mean.

10. Make periodic process checks.

Facilitators periodically stop the action to check on whether the meeting is still effective. Facilitators check if the purpose is still clear to everyone, if the process is working, if the pace is too fast or too slow, and to find out how people are feeling.

Effective Note Taking

Facilitation is closely identified with those awkward three-legged easels that are the trademark of the profession. Flip charts were invented by the first facilitators who were looking for a way to enable group members to track discussions as they unfolded.

Today, flip charts are quickly being eclipsed by all manner of electronic boards and digital displays. While this trend is likely to continue, don't be surprised if those awkward flip-chart stands stick around as well.

A lot of people dislike writing on flip charts. You may be one of them. You may also be wondering if it's really necessary to write on a flip chart or whiteboard when you're facilitating. The answer is yes, it really is important.

Writing on a flip chart lets people see immediate proof that their ideas have been heard. It also reassures them that their ideas have been captured. On top of that, writing on a flip chart or electronic board lets everyone in the room track progress. Using a flip chart or whiteboard also lets you use charts and grids. These tools provide needed structure during complex decision-making discussions.

Writing on a flip chart or electronic board requires using slightly larger handwriting so people can read the words from across the room. Lots of people try to get out of writing on a flip chart by claiming that their handwriting is a mess. Since very few people are able to create flawless flip charts, it's best to relax about both spelling and penmanship. Make apologies to your meeting attendees in advance, and ask them to accept that the most important aspect of recording ideas is to accurately capture key ideas.

The Rules of Wording

Since facilitators always strive to be neutral to ensure that group members control outcomes, it's important to accurately record what people say without editing too much. If you change too many words or add words that you personally prefer, group members will feel that you're just pretending to facilitate! The first rule of recording ideas is, therefore, to faithfully record what people are saying.

Since people say much more than can be recorded in a few crisp statements, facilitators are constantly challenged to create a short, concise summary of the dialogue. This is tricky, since it necessitates editing, which can lead to inadvertently changing what was said. This means that you have to become very good at editing while still remaining faithful to the original idea. Here are two simple rules to remember about recording group discussions:

Rule #1—Use their words. Listen carefully for the key words that participants use and ensure that these words are included in what gets written on the flip chart. Reinforce this by saying things like:

> *"I'm writing the word 'disaster' because you emphasized it."*
> *"Let me read you back what I wrote to check if I accurately captured your point."*

Rule #2—Ask permission to change words. If a participant rambles or can't find the right words, offer wording, but get member approval to ensure that what's recorded reflects what the person intended to say. Say something like:

> *"I've shortened what you said to . . . Is this okay?"*
> *"Can I use the word...?"*
> *"Is it okay to record that idea this way?"*

Recording Tip

A great technique to keep up your sleeve is to ask people to dictate the exact words they want to see recorded. This is useful if you don't understand what they're saying, or if you lost focus momentarily and can't remember what they said. In these situations say something like:

> *"Tell me what you want me to write down."*
> *"Give me the exact words you need to see on the board."*

This technique also works when people have shared long, convoluted ideas. Rather than taking on the task of creating a summary of their comments, ask them to take responsibility for doing this. Say something like:

> *"I want to be sure that I record the important parts of your idea.*
> *Give me one or two crisp sentences that capture what you just said."*

16

Communicating Caring

The bulk of this chapter has focused on the how-to aspects of facilitation. While learning to use these tools is certainly important, all the expertise in the world will not make you a great facilitator. No matter how proficient you are at using the core tools, you'll just be going through the motions if you don't communicate real caring to your clients. If this sounds a bit *touchy-feely*, remember that consulting is relationship intense. Your clients are placing a great deal of faith in you. In order to gain their trust, you need to convey your desire to help them achieve their goals.

That's why facilitation is such a critically important skill to master. When you ask questions, listen actively, paraphrase and make notes, it communicates that you care enough to want to understand everything about your clients and their goals.
When you deploy the structured conversations described in the second half of this book with a sincere sense of caring and concern for your clients, this approach will foster a real sense of collaboration and help you to build trusting partnerships.

Flip Chart Do's and Don'ts

DO	DON'T
Write down exactly what members say. If comments have to be edited, always use their key words. Check to make sure that what is written captures the meaning expressed.	Write down your personal interpretation of things. These are their notes. If unsure, ask, *"What should I write down?"*
Use verbs and make phrases fairly complete. For example, recording: "work group" is not as helpful as: "work group to meet Mondays at 10 a.m." Always be sure the notes make sense, even to someone who wasn't at the meeting.	Worry about spelling. If you make a fuss, it will inhibit members from getting up and taking a turn at facilitating.
Talk and write at the same time. This is necessary in order to maintain a good pace. Practiced facilitators can write one thing while asking the next question.	Hide behind the flip chart or talk to it. Unless you're writing, stand squarely beside it, facing the members when reading back notes.
Move around and act alive. There is nothing worse than a facilitator who seems to be chained to the flip chart. If an important point is being made, walk closer to the person who's talking so you can better pay attention.	Stand passively at the flip chart while a long discussion is going on without writing anything down. Ideas don't need to be in complete sentences before recording them. Make note of key words and ideas. Comprehensive statements can be formulated later.
Write in black, blue or some other dark color. Use fairly large letters so it can be read from the back of the room. Avoid red and pink markers.	Use print unless you have great handwriting. Avoid red and other pale pastels that are impossible to see from any distance.
Post flip chart sheets around the room so that people can keep track of what has been discussed.	Hide the pages with notes so that no one can reference the points already made.

Starting a Facilitation

Anyone who attends meetings knows that things can easily go off track or get stalled if there's confusion about the focus of a conversation. That's why facilitators ensure that there's always clarity regarding the scope of an agenda item before they let people plunge in. They create this clarity by using something called the *Start Sequence*. *Start Sequences* have the following three components:

The Start Sequence

---

1. The Purpose – Facilitators always start by making a statement that clearly describes the goal of the facilitated discussion. This is <u>what</u> will be discussed. This can take the form of a simple goal statement, or it can be more detailed and include a description of the desired outcomes.

2. The Process – They tell group members <u>how</u> the session will be conducted. This helps the participants understand how decisions will be made, the speaking order, and any structuring tools that will be used. The process description should also clarify if members are making the final decision or if they're simply being asked for input regarding a decision that will be made later by others.

3. The Timeframe – Facilitators tell people how long the entire discussion will take. In more complex conversations, timeframes should also be provided for each segment within the discussion.

During a Facilitation

Once a discussion is underway, it can easily get sidetracked or stuck, even when there's a clear *Start Sequence* in place. This can happen for any number of reasons, including:

- the topic may be more complex than anticipated
- the conversation may have drifted onto another topic
- the process tool being used may not be the right one for the discussion
- the original timeframes may not have been realistic
- individuals may be feeling tired or lose focus

Sometimes there are obvious signs that the discussion has become derailed, but there are also lots of times when there are few, if any, outward signs that meeting effectiveness has declined. That's why it's vitally important for facilitators to periodically stop the action and conduct what is known as a *Process Check*.

What's a *Process Check*?

Process checking is like taking the pulse of the group. Conducting a *Process Check* involves stopping the action to ask people how it's going.

The 4 P's of Process Checking

There are four basic areas of inquiry in Process Checking:
 	
    1. Progress
 	
    2. Process
 	
    3. Pace
 	
    4. People

1. Check for progress: Ask the members if they think the goal of the discussion is being achieved. Do they think that the purpose is still clear? Do they think that the conversation is still on topic?

When to check for progress: If few ideas are emerging, when the conversation goes in circles, at periodic intervals or at points of closure.

2. Check the process: Ask members if they feel that the tool or approach being used is working. Ask how much longer they're willing to keep using that tool or approach. Offer other tools to test if they want to switch approaches.

When to check the process: When the tool being used isn't yielding results, or when it's evident that the designated process isn't being followed or at periodic intervals.

3. Check the pace: Ask members if things are moving at the right pace. Ask if the pace is dragging, rushed or just right.

When to check the pace: When timelines are not being met, or at periodic intervals.

4. Check the people: Ask people how they're feeling. Ask if anyone feels frustrated, bored, tired, confused, etc.

When to check the people: When the meeting has been going on for a long time, when people grow silent and withdraw. When people yawn or look frustrated.

Ending a Facilitation

One of the biggest meeting pitfalls is ending without real closure or detailed next steps. When members leave a meeting without action plans, the entire gathering can feel like a waste of time.

Whether ending a one-hour meeting or an all-day marathon, facilitators always provide a summary of key points to ensure that there's a shared view of the outcome. Even if the session was a non-decision-making session, facilitators should provide a concise summary of what was discussed.

Ending a Non-Decision-Making Discussion:

At the end of a discussion during which people shared information, brainstormed ideas or made lists, it's a facilitator best practice to provide a summary of the points discussed. This allows people to add any points that were missed, and it brings closure.

Ending a Decision-Making Discussion:

At the end of a session during which group members made one or more decisions, the facilitator needs to recap what was decided to ratify the outcome and ensure that clear action steps are in place. This can include:

- reviewing the details of the decision
- checking the decision for clarity and completeness
- ratifying the decision by asking all members if they can live with the outcome to reduce the risks of post-meeting loss of commitment
- identifying next steps and creating detailed action plans

In addition to helping group members summarize and plan for action, facilitators also do some or all of the following to end a facilitation:

- Round up *Parking Lot* items and help members identify how to deal with them in the future.
- Help members create an agenda for their next meeting.
- Decide on a means of follow-up: written reports, emails, personal reports.
- Help members decide who will transcribe the flip chart sheets.
- Allow group members to take digital snapshots of flip charts if they have an immediate need for notes.
- Help members evaluate the session.
- Thank group members for their openness and participation.

Using Feedback to Continuously Improve

Facilitators believe that continuous feedback is essential to get a realistic picture of progress. The survey that follows is ideally implemented at the midpoint of a project to get member feedback about how it's going and what can be done to improve any items that receive poor ratings. If the survey is completed anonymously, you will get more accurate feedback than if you try to gather input in a meeting. Using a survey also allows you to gather input from stakeholders outside the immediate project team. This can include members of the board, senior managers, customers, strategic partners and employees affected by project outcomes. This will send your clients the message that you care about their satisfaction with how the project is being managed.

Project Diagnostic

Each survey will need to be custom designed depending on the stage of the project and the issues being encountered. Surveys can be sent out electronically and tabulated using survey data management software.

Once the survey results have been tabulated, you can use the *Survey-Feedback* process on page 106 to engage team members in dialogue to find improvement strategies.

Build your survey using a 1 to 5 scale.

1	2	3	4	5
Poor	Fair	Satisfactory	Good	Excellent

Some typical mid-point survey questions include:
- To what extent has a clear project goal been communicated to all stakeholders?
- Are the current project timelines realistic?
- Do we currently have the right people on the team?
- To what extent is the project staying on track?
- Are we reaching milestones on time?
- How effective are communications within the project team?
- How effective are communications between the team and key stakeholders?
- To what extent are you able to access the resources you need, when you need them?
- How well does the project team identify and solve problems?
- How would you rate the level of support that you're currently receiving?
- How effective is our team at identifying problems and resolving them?
- To what extent are we monitoring people's reactions to proposed changes?

The Best and Worst Practices of Facilitators

Some of the best things that a facilitator can do include:
- Carefully assess the needs of the members.
- Probe sensitively into people's feelings.
- Create an open and trusting atmosphere.
- Help people understand why they're there.
- View yourself as serving the group's needs.
- Make members the center of attention.
- Speak in simple and direct language.
- Work hard to stay neutral.
- Display energy and appropriate levels of assertiveness.
- Champion ideas you don't personally favor.
- Stay flexible and ready to change direction, if necessary.
- Listen intently to fully understand what's being said.
- Make notes that reflect what participants mean.
- Periodically gather related ideas into a coherent summary.
- Know how to use a wide range of process tools.
- Make sure every session ends with clear steps for the next meeting.
- Ensure that participants feel ownership for what has been achieved.
- End on a positive and optimistic note.

Some of the worst things a facilitator can do include:
- Remain oblivious to what the group thinks or needs.
- Never check member concerns.
- Fail to listen carefully to what's being said.
- Lose track of key ideas.
- Take poor notes or change the meaning of what's said.
- Try to be the center of attention.
- Get defensive.
- Get into personality battles.
- Put people down.
- Avoid or ignore conflict.
- Let a few people or the leader dominate.
- Never check how the meeting is going.
- Be overly passive on process.
- Push ahead on an irrelevant agenda.
- Have no alternate approaches.
- Let discussions get badly sidetracked.
- Let discussions ramble without proper closure.
- Be oblivious about when to stop.
- Be insensitive to cultural diversity issues.
- Use inappropriate humor.

Facilitation at a Glance Cue Card

To Start a Facilitation

- Welcome participants
- Introduce members
- Explain your role
- Clarify session goal
- Explain the process
- Set time frames
- Appoint a timekeeper
- Create a parking lot
- Start the discussion

Remember to:

- Stay neutral
- Listen actively
- Ask questions
- Paraphrase
- Record ideas
- Synthesize ideas
- Keep on track
- Test assumptions
- Provide summaries

During A Facilitation

- Check the purpose
- Check the process
- Check the pace
- Check the people

Conflict Management:

- Vent feelings
- Surface concerns
- Solve problems
- Redirect behaviors

To End a Facilitation

- Summarize discussions
- Clarify and ratify decisions
- Create action plans
- Round up leftover items
- Help create the next agenda
- Help group evaluate the meeting

Tookit:

- Visioning
- Forcefield Analysis
- Brainstorming
- Multi-voting
- Gap Analysis
- Risk Assessment
- Decision Grids
- Needs and Offers Dialogue
- Systematic Problem Solving

Chapter Two – Effective Questioning

Questions are the heart and soul of facilitation. They're the main technique for getting the client to open up, reflect, imagine, buy-in, identify problems and discover creative solutions.

It's important to understand that there's a lot more to good questioning than simply asking the first thing that pops into your head. Questions have structure and need to be carefully designed to ensure that they're sensitive and on target. That's why professional facilitators carefully plan the questions they're going to ask. Planning ensures that they're asking the right question, the right way, at the right time.

The Principles of Effective Questioning

One of the great challenges of questioning effectively is that there isn't a standard set of questions that works in every setting. A line of questioning that works really well with one client might confuse or upset another client. Even the questions contained in this chapter are only offered as food for thought. It's always important to remember that every question has to be carefully evaluated to ensure that it's appropriate. Keep these guidelines in mind:

1. **Customize for context:** Be sure that questions are sensitive to things like the client's organizational culture, occupational group, gender mix, values, environmental factors, financial situation, recent history and current stresses.

2. **Create inviting questions:** Avoid embedding too many of your own thoughts and suggestions inside questions. This will lead people to answers that you favor and will make you look manipulative. Ask the kind of open-ended questions that encourage deep, creative thought.

3. **Ask with sensitivity:** Unless you decide to deliberately confront your clients to shake them out of complacent thinking, questions should always be asked mindfully. That means avoiding harsh language and verbal traps that raise client anxiety and increase distrust. Maintaining positive body language is a big part of this too.

4. **Clarify assumptions:** Check out your understanding of what clients are saying. Sometimes they use language differently or understate how they really feel. Ask things like: *"Am I correct in thinking that...?" "Let me see if I've understood correctly that..."* or *"Are you saying that...?"*

Question Types

There are two basic question types: closed-ended and open-ended. Each has its uses, but facilitators predominantly use open-ended questions because they encourage clients to engage.

Type of Question	Description	Examples
Closed-ended	Elicits one-word answers and tends to close discussion	*"Does everyone understand the changes we've discussed?"*
	Solicits yes/no answers or ratings	*"Where is this on a scale of 1-5, with 5 being excellent?"*
	Useful to clarify and test assumptions	*"Have I given a clear description of the situation?"*
	Often begins with *"is,"* *"can,"* *"how many,"* or *"does"*	*"Does any of this need more elaboration?"*
Open-ended	Requires more than yes/no answers	*"What ideas do you have for explaining the changes to our customer?"*
	Stimulates thinking. Often begins with, or contains *"what," "how," "when,"* or *"why"*	*"If we were going to do something totally innovative, what would that look like?"*

Questioning Formats

The sample questions in this chapter are organized according to their intention. In addition, each question also represents one of the following questioning formats. You can use these various questioning structures to ensure that your facilitation work evokes a broad range of responses. Facilitators are always careful not to get in the rut of relying on just one type of question.

Fact-finding questions are targeted at verifiable data such as who, what, when, where and how much. Use them to gather information about the current situation.

> *"What kind of computer equipment are you using now?"*
> *"How much training did staff receive at the start of the project?"*

Feeling-finding questions ask for subjective information that gets at the participants' opinions, feelings, values and beliefs. They help you understand gut reactions.

> *"How do you feel about the new office layout?"*
> *"What kind of reaction are you expecting from the staff?"*

Tell-me-more questions encourage people to provide more details. They encourage people to elaborate.

> *"Tell me more."*
> *"Can you elaborate on that?"*
> *"What else comes to mind?"*

Best/worst questions help you understand potential opportunities in the present situation. They let you test for the outer limits of participants' wants and needs.

> *"What's the best thing about switching software?"*
> *"What's the worst thing about a software change?"*

Third-party questions help uncover thoughts in an indirect manner. They allow people to speculate on what others might think, without challenging them to reveal their personal thoughts.

> *"Do you have any thoughts about why some people might resist this idea?"*
> *"Why would a team member not want to attend a team-building session?"*

Magic wand questions help you explore people's desires. Also known as crystal ball questions, these are useful to temporarily remove obstacles from a person's mind.

> *"If money were no object, which software would you buy?"*
> *"If you had total control over the project, what would you change?"*

The Importance of Follow-on Questions

One of the most important aspects of effective questioning is the ability to ask the right follow-on questions. Follow-on questioning matters because the initial reply to a question often fails to get to the underlying issue. Think of follow-on questioning as *"peeling the onion"* to get to the heart of what's really going on. Some lines of questioning may need to be pursued three or four times to get to the core issue.

While the exact wording of follow-on questions can't be predicted, there are some general principles to keep in mind:

1. Start with straightforward fact-finding questions.

2. Follow up with questions that clarify the initial responses.

3. Ask for the rationale behind those responses.

4. Ask how things unfolded.

5. Use feeling-finding questions to get at the emotions buried at the core of the matter.

6. Use third-party or magic wand questions in case people are blocked.

Asking Sensitive Questions

Other than those rare instances when a group needs to be deliberately confronted in order to avoid a catastrophe, facilitators work hard to avoid anything that feels threatening. When a line of questioning touches on a sensitive topic, facilitators often allow people to write their responses on pieces of paper. These are collected and tabulated before being shared, to ensure group member safety. This is especially true when questions press people to disclose information of a personal nature.

Here are some ways to safely ask tough questions:

- Create an anonymous way to gather data. This can be a paper survey that respondents return in a sealed envelope, a reply that they send via email to your office only, or an anonymous reply on an automated survey form.
- Use slips of paper. Allow a few minutes for quiet reflection and writing. Have people pass their notes to you. Mix them up and read them aloud without reference to who made which comment.
- Pose sensitive questions with a 1-5 rating scale on a flip chart or whiteboard. Invite people to write their rating on a slip of paper, collect these and post the ratings. No one will know who gave which scores.
- Place a question and rating scale on a flip chart. Allow time for people to write their score on a slip of paper. Turn the flip chart toward a corner and

invite people to file by one at a time to post their answers. Brave people will go first, while those who feel most nervous will wait to post their ideas and ratings after there are several numbers already on the board. Turn the board around to share the ratings.

The Question Bank

On the following pages you'll find samples of questions facilitators routinely ask. To make them more relevant, they've been reframed to fit a consulting context. The best way to use these sample questions is to think of them as food for thought.

Many of the sample questions can be used *"off the shelf,"* although they will be more effective if they're adapted to fit the context. While most questions are asked in the moment, note that it's often a good idea to send questions to group members in advance so that they have time to reflect and prepare appropriate answers. These questions can be used in groups, on surveys and one-on-one.

Questions to Get to Know the Client

"Tell me the story of the organization."

"What would you say was the organization's outstanding strength/achievement?"

"What's the organization's image with the public?"

"What values drive this organization?"

"Is your organization's culture generally receptive to outside input and to making major change?"

"Does the organization work through departmental silos, or do people work cross-functionally?"

"When a change is being contemplated, does management deliberately seek out employee input?"

"Does the organization have a peer feedback or upward feedback process?"

"What would your most satisfied customers say about you?"

"What words would your main competitors use to describe you?"

"Is there anything about the organization that an outsider like me might find confusing/surprising?"

"What has been the organization's major turning points/challenges, and how were they handled?"

"Who has been most instrumental in making the organization a success?"

"What role have you played in that success?"

"What would you guess were the things that the people who work here are most proud of?"

"What's the greatest strength of the people inside this company?"

"If you had a magic wand, what one thing would you change immediately?"

"If you could turn back the hands of time, what one event would you go back and change?"

"Rate the current organizational state on a scale of 1-10, with 10 representing an ideal state."

"Imagine that it's exactly ten years from today and there's a really positive headline in the newspaper about this organization. What does that headline say?"

Questions to Clarify the Consultant-Client Relationship

"Tell me about your past experience with external consultants. How might those experiences affect our work?"

"What's the number one skill or talent that you're hoping I bring to the project? What are the second and third?"

"What's the best contribution that I can make to this project?"

"Describe your idea of the ideal consultant/client relationship?"

"What powers do you think I will need to be able to manage the various challenges that could crop up?"

"Who should I be talking to on a regular basis? Are there any parties I shouldn't communicate with directly?"

Questions to Help People Get to Know One Another

"If you had to condense your resume down to four sentences, what would they be?"

"Give us a single snapshot from your youth that tells us who you are today."

"Tell us one interesting thing about your hometown/ youth/ college years?"

"Tell us the three main things/events/talents that got you to where you are today?"

"Complete this sentence: My ultimate career destiny is to…?"

"What's the hidden talent, past experience or hobby most people here don't know about you?"

"What's the most enjoyable part of your job?"

"What part of your current job do you find most challenging?"

"If you had to name one additional skill or bit of education you'd like to acquire, what would it be?"

"What unique gift, experience or skill do you bring to this organization/project/ team?"

"What would your colleagues say was your main contribution to the workplace?"

"What motivates you to do a great job?"

"What traits do you most need to see in a leader? In a fellow team member?"

"If you could invite three thoughtful people or leaders in your field to be part of this team, whom would you ask and why?"

Questions to Assess the Current Situation

"What are the things that this organization does exceedingly well?"

"What are the things that this organization does just okay?"

"What are the things that this organization does poorly?"

"What's going on in the environment that this organization needs to be especially aware of? What about competitors, suppliers, customers, finances, materials, human resources, machinery, etc.?"

"Does the organization have a systematic way of evaluating effectiveness, such as an organized process-improvement program?"

"What are the current barriers to working effectively that we need to pay attention to? Are there communication barriers? Is it difficult to access resources/get approvals, etc.?"

"Given the current situation, what are all the possible approaches you suspect organizational change experts might recommend?"

"What are the consequences for the organization if this project fails?"

"What would be the best possible outcome of this project?"

"If you had to give me one piece of helpful advice, what would it be?"

Questions to Establish Project Parameters

"What are some of the guidelines you've worked with in other projects that you think we should also adopt?"

"Do all projects undergo an initial cost/benefit analysis?"

"How will we make decisions? Who can decide what?"

"Which types of decisions need to be a consensus?"

"How should we communicate about work in progress, problems and issues?"

"How do we avoid starting a rumor mill about possible changes?"

"What are the guidelines about who can talk to whom about what?"

"What's the process for missing a deadline or overshooting the budget?"

"How can we always ensure that resources are fairly allocated? What's the process if this doesn't happen?"

"How often do we need to meet to update project status?"

"How often do I need to report? What form should my reports take?"

"What should we consider to be an emergency? What sub-routines should we establish to ensure that these are handled effectively?"

Questions to Establish Behavioral Norms or Rules of Conduct

"Think back to a time when you worked on a team where everybody got along. What attitudes and behaviors did people exhibit? What rules did they follow?"

"What one helpful thing have you learned working on other projects and teams that you think this group should consider making a rule for this project?"

"List the top five things that motivate you in terms of how you're treated by both leaders and colleagues. Which of these need to become part of how this team operates?"

"What's the best way to head off or avoid interpersonal conflicts or disputes?"

"What kinds of information can we share, and what information needs to stay inside the group?"

"What can we do to ensure that confidentiality is maintained with respect to sensitive information?"

"What should the rule be about people missing project meetings?"

"What's the best rule for checking emails during a meeting?"

"How should we handle the good times we might encounter as a team? How about the bad times?"

"Under what conditions would you be willing to give and receive feedback about both team and personal performance?"

Questions to Identify Expectations

"Imagine that today is the last meeting of this project and that it was successful beyond your wildest dreams! What would we be celebrating today?"

"In your own words answer the question, 'Why are we here?' "

"What's the burning question that absolutely must be addressed by this project?"

"What are the specific deliverables that need to be accomplished? By what dates?"

"If we asked employees for their hopes for this project, what would they say?"

"If we asked your competition what they would most like to see come out of this project, what would they say?"

"If we could get only two positive outcomes from this entire initiative, what should they be?"

"What do you think employees are hoping to gain from the changes that will emerge from this project?"

"What are the important milestones on the way to a successful outcome?"

"Describe the most positive thing you could personally gain from this project."

"How will we know if we've been successful or unsuccessful?"

Questions to Uncover Issues or Problems

"Describe the biggest problem that this project could encounter, as a one-line newspaper headline."

"If we encounter scope creep, why is it most likely to occur?"

"Could we potentially encounter any ethical issues during this project? What are they?"

"What catastrophic event could cause this project to lose its funding or lose management support?"

"Is there anyone or any group that might benefit from our failure to complete this project?"

"Name a factor outside of our control that is adversely affecting our project."

"What's working/not working right now?"

"If you had to rank the top three issues being encountered in order of priority, what would they be?"

"How can we improve our capacity to notice issues and deal with them quickly?"

"Are there any recurring patterns in relation to this issue?"

"Are we looking at the whole picture, or are we seeing just one small part of something larger?"

"Can you describe fully what's happening with respect to this issue?"

"As an important member of this project, what keeps you awake at night?"

"Are there areas within the organization where commitment or capacity might be a concern?"

"What resources can we draw on in times of trouble? How can we build bridges to these resources now? Whom do we need to call on for each type of problem we might encounter?"

Questions to Encourage Creative Thinking

"How would other cultures approach this challenge? What would the Japanese do? The Germans? The Swedes?"

"If we think revolution instead of evolution, how does that change things?"

"If we set out to delight customers instead of just meet their needs, what would that look like?"

"What other companies have totally transformed themselves? What did they do?"

"What external resources can the people inside this organization call on?"

"What questions haven't we asked ourselves?"

"Describe some of the most innovative products or approaches to service that you know of. What makes them special?"

"What's the most obvious solution? What's the least obvious?"

"What would we do if money were no object?"

"What would your biggest competitors want you to do?"

"What's the opposite of what we plan to do? Is there an element of that which we need to consider?"

"What have you never done before that we ought to put on the table?"

"What would an 8-year-old say? What would an 80-year-old say?"

Questions to Assess Resistance to Change

"What are the biggest challenges inherent in our strategy? What stands in our way?"

"What are the biggest external threats that could crop up and hinder our efforts?"

"What is it that people argue most about inside this organization?"

"Is there an aspect of this organization's culture that could factor in blocking change?"

"What is it that most frustrates the people working inside this company?"

"What types of changes do people typically resist? Which of these are we most likely to encounter?"

"Think back to a big project that you worked on before. What roadblocks did you run into?"

"How do you think employees are going to react to this change on a purely gut level?"

Complete this sentence: "The thing that could come out of left field and blindside us is…"

"Who are some of the key players, and how might they each react to change?"

"If people are going to resist our recommendations, who's most likely to do that and what form will the resistance take?"

"What are all the factors that we need to consider that might have an impact on successful implementation?"

Questions to Identify Implications

"Let's look at the main ideas on the table and drill down to identify the impacts of each on the project and the organization."

"If we go ahead as planned, what are the expected outcomes? What are some of the potential unanticipated things we could encounter?"

"What are the potential impacts of downsizing/scaling up/adding a new product/ moving to a new location?"

"Look into a crystal ball and tell me what you see that could be an unexpected implication."

"What's one thing we know for sure about the bottom line on this matter?"

Questions to Build Ownership and Commitment

"What is the biggest potential gain for the company? For you personally?"

"What do you personally hope to contribute to this initiative?"

"What will ensure that every single employee gets on board to help make change a reality?"

"What do you feel is the biggest hope that individual employees have with respect to this change?"

"What's the most important factor for getting senior management solidly on our team?"

"What outcome will most ensure that your strategic business partners continue their commitment to you?"

Questions to Prompt for Clarity

"Could you be more specific?"

"Can you say that another way?"

"Please say a little more about that."

"Can you give us another example?"

"What's the opposite of that?"

"Could someone please restate that idea to make sure we all understand this the same way?"

"Tell us all more. How does this impact us?"

Questions to Gain Perspective

"Has anyone experienced a similar situation?"

"What assumptions are we making about this idea?"

"What are the pros and cons of this idea?"

"If we've forgotten one thing, what is it?"

"If this team had a blind spot, what would it be?"

"How might other stakeholders see this issue?"

"How are employees/customers going to react?"

"Let's think of just one more perspective on this so that we can capture another point of view."

"Does anyone have something totally different to suggest?"

Questions to Challenge and Confront

"In what way is our current strategy basically what you've always done?"

"If you had to identify one reason why this project hasn't gone as far as it should or been as bold as it needed to be, what would that be?"

"If there was one human trait that's holding this project back, what would you say it was?"

"How could our actions potentially get in the way of follow-through on change plans?"

"How does the organization contribute to the problem? How do we?"

The final question to ask when you sense that there's still something that hasn't been brought to the surface:

"What's the one question that we haven't asked ourselves yet?"

> **If you want to improve your facilitation skills, check out our online course!**
>
> **Get the details on page 121.**

Questioning Do's and Don'ts

DO	DON'T
Ask clear, concise questions covering a single issue.	Ask rambling, ambiguous questions that cover multiple issues.
Ask a good combination of questions.	Get stuck asking only fact-finding questions.
Retool questions to fit the context.	Ask every client the same questions.
Ask challenging questions that will stimulate thought.	Ask questions without providing an opportunity for thought.
Use mostly open-ended questions.	Forget that closed-ended questions can be useful for testing understanding.
Ask questions that are sensitive to feelings.	Ask trick questions designed to entrap or fool people.
Ask reasonable questions based on what people know.	Ask questions that most people can't answer.
Ask honest and relevant questions.	Ask questions that lead people to the answer you want.
Ask appropriate follow-on questions to get to the heart of the matter.	Assume that the first answer people offer is the only facet of the issue.

Chapter Three –
Focus on Decision Making

One of the most difficult things to do is to help a group of people arrive at a joint decision that everyone can live with. Group decision making is difficult because:

- People often have their minds made up and consequently spend all their time promoting their ideas without considering alternatives.
- Some people have an argumentative style that leads them to become strident or use emotional language.
- The complexity of an issue may be underestimated, resulting in a discussion that lacks sufficient exploration.
- The group may be coming to the decision-making session without sufficient information or lacking the technical expertise needed to be able to make the right decision.
- When the decision-making discussion is unstructured, conversations tend to go in circles or miss important elements.

This last point is actually the main motivation behind this book, which is to provide clear, step-by-step guidance for complex group decision-making discussions. Years of research into group dynamics has shown conclusively that decision-making conversations involving more than three people are extremely ineffective when they're unstructured.

It's important to note that there's a direct correlation between decision-making methods and the tools used to resolve conflict. Many conflicts rise to the surface during decision-making discussions, because people have differing views. Because there's such a direct link between decision making and conflict management, you will find page references throughout this chapter and the next to highlight how various tools support each other.

Conversation Structures

Before delving into the techniques for making group decisions, it's important that you understand that there are two types of facilitated conversations: they are either decision making in nature or they are not. Each type of conversation has distinct features that dictate the techniques used to manage them.

Non-Decision-Making Conversations

Non-decision-making conversations are those in which group members simply share ideas or information. During non-decision-making discussions, the facilitator simply records all ideas without checking with others to test if they concur.

Examples of non-decision-making conversations include:

- A brainstorming session in which all ideas are accepted and not judged
- An information-sharing session in which group members describe their experiences or update each other
- A relationship-building session in which people get to know each other
- A discussion aimed at making a list of individual preferences or key factors in a situation

In non-decision-making conversations, all ideas are recorded without being filtered. Sometimes, these ideas are ranked and sorted later.

Decision-Making Conversations

Decision-making conversations are those discussions in which group member ideas are combined to arrive at either an action plan or a rule that group members feel they can accept and implement.

Facilitators need to manage decision-making conversations differently than non-decision-making ones, since they need to help members reach agreement. This involves clarifying ideas, ping-ponging ideas around so others can add their thoughts, making statements that summarize the discussion and recording the group opinion.

Examples of decision-making discussions:

- Deciding between two alternatives
- Creating group norms or rules of conduct for a meeting
- Building a compromise solution that everyone can live with
- Developing joint solutions to a problem

Non-Decision-Making	Decision Making

- Conversations in which no action plans or norms are identified or ratified. Examples include:
  - Information sharing
  - Brainstorming
  - List making
	- Discussions in which action plans or rules are identified and ratified

	- Discussions where members arrive at a joint decision
- One-way dialogue	- Interactive dialogue
- The facilitator records individual ideas	- The facilitator records group opinions

The Decision-Making Options

Whenever you need to help a group make a decision, you can use one of five distinct decision-making methods. Each of these options represents a different approach. Each has pros and cons. A decision option should always be chosen carefully to be sure it fits. Examples showing exactly how to use these approaches are provided throughout Section Two of this book. In each Structured Conversation, you will be given guidance about when and how to use the five decision options described below.

The Five Decision Options

- Building a consensus through joint analysis and brainstorming
- Making lists and then using multi-voting to prioritize options
- Building a compromise option to bridge the gap between two positions
- Using majority voting to decide between competing options
- Appointing an expert to make a final decision that's binding on the group

---

Consensus Building

*Consensus building creates participation and
buy-in to the generated solutions.*

Consensus building means ensuring that everyone has a clear understanding of the situation or issue to be decided, analyzing all of the relevant facts together and then jointly developing solutions that represent the whole group's best thinking about the optimal decision. Consensus building is characterized by a lot of listening, healthy debate and testing of options. Consensus generates a decision about which everyone says, *"I can live with it."*

Pros - It's a collaborative effort that unites the group. It demands high involvement. It's systematic, objective and fact-driven. It builds buy-in and high commitment to the outcome.

Cons - It's time-consuming and produces low-quality decisions when done without proper data collection or if the wrong people are in the room.

Uses - When a decision will impact the entire group, when buy-in and ideas from all members are essential and/or when the importance of the decision being made is worth the time it will take to complete the consensus process.

Steps – Name the issue, topic or problem. Share all of the known facts to create a shared understanding of the current situation. Generate potential courses of action/solutions. Generate criteria for sorting the courses of action/solutions. Use the criteria to sort the ideas (can be a decision grid, vote or multi-vote). Make a clear statement of the decision. Ratify that all can live with the solution. Identify action plans.

An example of a consensus-building session can be found on page 101. Also see the steps of collaborative problem solving on page 50.

Multi-Voting

> Multi-voting is a kind of voting activity that's useful when
> there are a lot of options or a lot of people involved.

Multi-voting is a priority-setting tool that's useful for making decisions when the group must select from multiple options. In these instances, rank ordering the options using a set of criteria will identify the best course of action.

> **Pros** - It's systematic, objective, democratic, noncompetitive and participative. Everyone wins somewhat, and feelings of loss are minimal. It's a fast way of sorting out a complex set of options. Tends to feel consensual.

> **Cons** - It's often associated with limited discussion, hence, limited understanding of the options. It can force choices on people who may not be satisfied, if their priorities did not rise to the surface. Sometimes people are swayed by each other if the voting is done out in the open, rather than electronically or by secret ballot.

> **Uses** - When there's a long list of alternatives or items to choose from.

> **Steps** - After the group has generated a wide range of solutions, clarify the criteria that define the votes (most important, easiest, least expensive, greatest impact, etc.). If using stickers, hand out strips of dots. If using markers, tell people how many marks to make. If using points, clarify how many points people can distribute (10 /100, etc.) Allow people to mill as they affix their votes.

Examples of multi-voting being used are on pages 77, 87, 90, 99, 101, 104 and 113.

Compromise

> Compromise involves finding a middle position
> between two opposing options.

Compromise is a negotiated approach that's applicable when there are two or more distinct options and members are strongly polarized (neither side is willing to accept the solution or position put forth by the other side). A middle position is then created that incorporates ideas from both sides. Throughout the process of negotiation, everyone wins a few points, but they also lose favored items. The outcome, therefore, is something that no one is totally satisfied with. In compromises, no one feels they got exactly what they wanted, so the emotional reaction is often, "*It's not really what I wanted, but I'm going to have to live with it.*"

Pros - It generates lots of discussion and does create a solution.

Cons - Negotiating when people are pushing a favored point of view tends to be adversarial, hence this approach divides the group. In the end, everyone wins, but everyone also loses.

Uses - When two opposing solutions are proposed, neither of which is acceptable to everyone; or when the group is strongly polarized and compromise is the only alternative.

Steps - Invite the two parties to give a description of the solution or course of action that they favor. Ask one party to make notes and then give a short summary of the solution or position favored by the other group. Engage the entire group in identifying the strengths and weaknesses of each proposed approach. Bring forward the strengths of both approaches. Create a third option or hybrid that builds on the strengths of both positions. Ask each group to willingly give up some aspects of their original approach in order to arrive at a decision that represents a middle ground. Clarify, summarize and ratify the middle-ground approach. Compromise can be win/win.

Refer to page 52 for a step-by-step description of how to facilitate a win/win compromise.

Majority Voting

This involves asking people to choose the option they favor, once clear choices have been identified. Usual methods are a show of hands or secret ballot. The quality of voting is always enhanced if there's good discussion to share ideas before a vote is taken.

> The quality of any voting exercise increases dramatically
> if it's preceded by a thorough discussion.

Pros - It's fast, and decisions can be high quality if the vote is preceded by a thorough analysis.

Cons - It can be too fast, and low in quality, if people vote based on their personal feelings without the benefit of hearing each other's thoughts or facts. It creates winners and losers, hence dividing the group. The show of hands method may put pressure on people to conform.

Uses - When there are two distinct options, if a decision must be made quickly and if a division in the group is acceptable. Use it mostly to make trivial decisions or to take the pulse of the group.

Steps - Ask members to describe both options in some detail to build a shared understanding. Identify criteria for deciding which is more effective (timeliness, cost, impact, etc.). Once everyone understands both options, and the criteria for deciding, use a show of hands or paper vote to identify which option to implement.

There are no examples of majority voting in Section Two of this book because it is not the optimal way to help a group reach a decision since it causes division.

One Person Decides

This is a decision that the group decides to empower one person to make on behalf of the members. A common misconception among teams is that every decision needs to be made by the whole group. In some situations, a one-person decision is not only faster, but a more effective way to get resolution. The quality of any one-person decision will be raised considerably if the person making the decision gets input from the other group members before deciding.

> Many groups ignore the fact that many decisions
> are best made by one person.

Pros - It's fast and accountability is clear. Can result in commitment and buy-in if people feel their ideas are represented.

Cons - It can divide the group if the person deciding doesn't consult the group or makes a decision that others can't live with. A one-person decision typically lacks in both the buy-in and synergy that come from a group decision-making process.

Uses - When there's a clear expert in the group, when only one person has the information needed to make a decision and can't share it, when one person is solely accountable for the outcome, or when the issue is unimportant or small.

Steps - Identify the expert who's best qualified to make the decision. To build buy-in, conduct a consultation during which group members tell the expert about their needs and concerns regarding the item to be decided. Gain agreement that everyone will accept the decision of the expert.

Each option has its place, so choose the most appropriate
method before each decision-making session.

Decision Options Summary Chart

Option	Pros	Cons	Uses
Consensus Building	Collaborative, systematic, participative, discussion-oriented, encourages commitment	Takes time, requires data and member skills	Important issues, when total buy-in matters
Multi-Voting	Systematic, objective, participative, feels like a win	Limits dialogue, influences choices, real priorities may not surface	To sort or prioritize a long list of options
Compromise	Discussion, creates a solution	Adversarial, win/lose, divides the group	When positions are polarized, when consensus is improbable
Majority Voting	Fast, high quality with dialogue, clear outcome	May be too fast, winners and losers, influenced choices	Trivial matter, if division of group is acceptable
One Person Decides	Can be fast, clear accountability	Lack of input, low buy-in, no synergy	When one person is the expert, individual willing to take sole responsibility

Always be aware of the impact of each method on group unity.

Chapter Four – Facilitating Through Conflict

Every project presents the potential for conflict. People can compete over resources, argue about strategies, clash over work styles or simply dislike each other. When conflict is unresolved, it can spiral out of control and hamper progress.

Fortunately there are useful tools that can help resolve even the thorniest issue. These techniques are never confrontational. Instead, they've been designed to reduce tensions and keep the parties safe. Each conflict tool described in this chapter adheres to certain guidelines. They all...

- approach conflict situations with the positive intention of finding solutions and repairing relationships
- rely heavily on core facilitation practices like active listening, paraphrasing and summarizing
- use behaviorally descriptive language that avoids naming or blaming
- seek to find positive solutions that everyone can live with
- use facilitator neutrality to avoid becoming personally embroiled in the conflict

Ineffective conflict management	Effective conflict management
- ambushing people	- gaining buy-in
- lashing out	- using respectful language
- name calling	- attacking issues instead of people
- dredging up the past	- looking forward
- talking at others	- talking with others
- I win/you lose	- we can work it out
- I'm right/you're wrong	- solutions we can both live with
- I look good/you look bad	- we both save face
- making someone lose face	- compassion
- punishment	- reconciliation
- burning bridges	- building bridges

Tackling conflict is always stressful and somewhat risky. If you use proven conflict-management techniques, however, your chances of successful resolution are greatly enhanced. On the following pages are some techniques worth learning.

Technique #1 – Preventing Conflict

In the same way that an ounce of prevention is worth a pound of cure, it's always best to create an environment where conflict is less likely to happen in the first place. One way to do this is to engage the groups you work with in setting rules that define how people ought to interact.

In behavioral science terms this is known as setting norms. Norms are rules or guidelines that describe how people will behave or how things will get done. These rules can be created anytime a problem occurs, but are more powerful when created to head off problems before they crop up.

You can use *Norming* to prevent conflict by helping a group create rules of conduct. This is especially powerful when you engage people in setting rules for situations that are anticipated to cause problems in the future. Used in this way, *Norming* becomes a preventive strategy.

We all know that simply setting rules doesn't guarantee harmony, but at least they provide a starting point. The process is easy. Rules or guidelines can be created at a meeting or before groups ever meet via email. Whether the rules are created in a face-to-face conversation or at a distance, the process is always the same: You simply ask specific *Norming* questions, and then ratify the answers that people provide. Examples of *Norming* questions can be found on the next page and also on pages 32 and 33.

Norming is also an important tool to use after a conflict or problem has occurred. In this setting, ask members to suggest rules that will help to ensure that a similar type of incident will never happen again.

When a group has a clear set of rules, anyone can point out if a rule is being ignored. This shares responsibility for maintaining a healthy climate.

Norming is extremely simple, but don't let its simplicity fool you. A set of rules that everyone has agreed to honor is a powerful tool for preventing strife. On the next page are some examples of *Norming* questions for a variety of situations. Notice that the person posing the questions is asking very detailed questions aimed at eliciting specific and clear rules.

Norming Questions to Generate Rules for Effective Meetings

"What can we do, at all our meetings to ensure that we always have healthy debates, instead of heated arguments? What specific behaviors would help?"

"What should we do anytime a conversation gets stuck and we start spinning in nonproductive circles?"

"What is it okay for any one of us to say if someone's presentation goes on for too long?"

"What rule do you want to have about side-chatting during meetings?"

"What should the rule be about coming and going during meetings?"

"What should the rule be about texting and working on laptops while we're discussing an agenda item?"

"What is it okay for any of us to say if we notice someone breaking one of our rules during a meeting?"

For an example of a typical set of meeting norms see page 68.

Safety Norms

If you're going to facilitate a discussion that requires a degree of disclosure and that might make people feel hesitant, post a set of norms designed specifically to make people feel safe. Write the starter set below on a flip-chart sheet or whiteboard. Leave space for additional rules. Read the starter list to the group so that they understand what you're looking for. Then, have each person pick a partner. Allow about five minutes, then ask the partners to report on any additional rules they would like to add. Add these to the list, and then ratify them with the whole group.

- What's said in the room stays in the room
- No naming or blaming
- Instead of criticizing, offer constructive suggestions
- Focus on finding solutions and moving forward
- Anyone who needs a break can suggest one to the group

Safety norms are essential for conversations such as those on pages 87, 99, 101, 104, 108, 111 and 115.

Technique # 2 – Collaborating to Solve a Problem

One of the most important conflict-resolution techniques to master is the art of getting people together to jointly find a solution that works for everyone. When the parties in a dispute start with a clean sheet of paper and blend their ideas to arrive at a way forward, the result will be an action plan that everybody can live with.

This technique is designed to be used when people are at odds about a specific situation or are encountering a problem. They might be fighting over scarce resources or arguing about who has the optimal solution for a particular problem.

Collaborating to resolve a conflict involves following an orderly series of steps in which the issue, block or barrier is jointly analyzed by those involved. Everyone offers ideas to resolve the matter and the proposed solutions are judged against objective criteria, rather than by subjective judgment. By the time the parties have arrived at a course of action, everyone will feel committed to the outcome since they've had a hand in its creation.

The main drawback to collaborating is that it takes time. This will feel like a waste of energy if it's used to resolve something trivial. Despite this, collaborating is the preferred approach to resolve any impasse where it's important to find solutions that also strengthen relationships.

Here are the steps of collaborative problem solving. Note that these steps can be used with a single person or with a group.

Step 1 - Set the stage
Step 2 - Clarify the issue
Step 3 - Set the ground rules for the discussion
Step 4 - Analyze the facts of the current situation
Step 5 - Work together to generate possible solutions
Step 6 - Evaluate the solutions
Step 7 - Select the optimal solution for both parties
Step 8 - Plan for action

Step 1 – Set the stage: Be sure that everyone is ready to look for solutions. Open the dialogue with an expression of your positive intentions:

> *"I'm optimistic that we can find a solution that works for all of us."*

Step 2 – Clarify the issue: Make a statement that describes the issue at the center of the dispute. You can make this statement or invite a participant to make the statement that clarifies the issue.

> *"Someone make a statement that describes the issue we're resolving."*

Step 3 – Set ground rules for the discussion: Agree to rules that will keep the conversation from turning into an argument. Discuss the behaviors that will ensure that it's a healthy debate.

> *"How do we keep this discussion from getting heated?"*
> *"How do we ensure that we listen with an open mind?"*
> *"How can we ensure the solution works equally for everyone?"*

Step 4 – Analyze the facts of the situation: Invite everyone to share what they know about the current situation/problem. Listen actively, paraphrase what others say, summarize key points. Don't allow anyone to disagree or to jump ahead to solutions. This ensures that people will really hear each other.

> *"What happened? Why did this happen? What contributed to the problem? How long has it been going on? Who else contributed to the problem? Who else was affected by the problem? Why hasn't it already been solved? What's been tried?"*

Step 5 – Work together to generate possible solutions: Once everyone has the same understanding of the current situation and sees the perspective of the others, it's time to list a range of possible solutions. Try to avoid the pitfall of having only one possible solution. If a number of ideas are brainstormed, this keeps people from getting locked into a single solution.

> *"What are all the possible solutions for this issue? What could we try? What haven't we tried before? What would be a really creative solution to this? What if money were no object? What if we had a magic wand?"*

Step 6 – Evaluate the solutions: Identify criteria for sorting through the brainstormed ideas. This could be easiest to do, least disruptive, least costly, best place to start, etc. You can use multi-voting or a decision grid to sort ideas.

> *"What are the most important criteria for sorting the potential solutions?"*

Step 7 – Ratify support for the selected solutions: Once you've helped the group members apply the criteria to sort the potential solutions, make a clear statement about the chosen path forward. Then check with everyone to make sure that they can live with the outcomes.

> *"Now that we have a solution, I want to check in with each of you to make sure that you can live with this outcome."*

Step 8 – Plan for action: Decide what will happen next. To make sure that there's a real commitment to taking action, set a date to check back on progress. This adds an element of accountability to the process.

> *"What are the next steps? How will we make that happen?"*

"When will each step be completed? Who's doing what?"
"When and how will we check in to make sure that we've followed through?"

Whenever the parties in a dispute sit down to solve a problem together, the result is a solution that reflects everyone's input. This gives the whole team a sense of ownership in the outcome: that's what builds consensus and creates an action plan that's likely to be implemented. Collaborating to solve a problem in this way will not only resolve the issue, but also improve relationships.

Refer to page 101 to see detailed process notes for a problem-solving meeting.

Technique # 3 – Building a *Win/Win Compromise*

Sometimes we encounter situations in which there are two opposing options. Person A likes his idea but really dislikes the idea proposed by the other person. Similarly, Person B likes her solution but hates that of Person A. When these folks get together, they each tout their own idea and barely listen to what the other person is saying. Often they get stuck, unwilling to budge.

When this happens, you need to find a new option that's halfway between what each party wants. This means that neither of them is going to get exactly what they want. Instead, they will each get some of the things they want but will have to give up other things in return.

The classic game of win/lose compromise is a maneuver in which each party tries to get the other party to give up more than they intended, while keeping more of what they wanted in the first place. In other words, each party tries to win while ensuring that the other party loses.

Below is a short description of how most people approach the classic *"I win/you lose"* type of compromise. If you've ever haggled over the price of a new car, you'll recognize this game.

- You start by overstating what you want so that you have something to give up later.
- You hide your real feelings and pretend that every part of your position is vitally important.
- You argue that your ideas are superior and essential, but that the other person's ideas are ridiculous and impractical.
- You bluff, make threats, act upset, threaten to walk out.
- You give the bare minimum with great reluctance.
- You haggle back and forth, hoping the other person gives in.
- You take the best deal you can get for yourself and leave.

The positive thing about this classic compromise technique is that it does eventually yield an outcome. The problem is that this traditional approach to building a consensus is devastating to relationships. By the time a compromise has been reached, both parties have been lied to, bluffed and somewhat bullied with the result that relationships are strained.

Win/Win Compromise is Different

Fortunately, there's a way to build a middle position that doesn't devastate relationships and that creates an outcome that feels like a win for both parties. The *Win/Win* approach is based on the idea that both parties should feel that they have won somewhat. To do this, use the following set of steps:

> Step 1 – Set the stage for *Win/Win.*
> Step 2 – Have the parties take turns describing their positions.
> Step 3 – Ask each party to become a champion for what the other party wants.
> Step 4 – Generate a list of common interests to foster a sense of unity.
> Step 5 – Zero in on what's most important for each party.
> Step 6 – Build an option that includes what matters most to each party.

Step 1 – Set the stage for *Win/Win*: Invite both parties to work on developing a compromise with you. Assure them that this is going to be an open and honest discussion to find a middle ground that works for everyone. Assure both parties that keeping the relationship strong is of paramount importance. Suggest the rules that everyone will present their positions without resorting to exaggerations, and that each party will listen respectfully to the ideas of the other party without refuting their points.

> *"I know that you each have a solution in mind and that you don't necessarily find each other's recommendations appealing. I'm going to ask you to keep an open mind for the duration of this meeting while we explore the possibility of finding a way forward that works for both of you. To do this, we need to listen to the opposing point of view without judgment, so please no rebutting or counter-arguing. This is really going to help."*

Step 2 – Let the parties take turns describing their separate positions: Flip a coin. Tell the first person to give a factual presentation. Ask the listener to make eye contact, maintain neutral body language and listen without judgment. When Person A is finished presenting, ask Person B to give a summary of the key points made. If Person A is satisfied, then Person B can ask clarifying questions. Repeat the process with Person B. Make notes on a flip chart while each person presents their proposal.

> *"Person A, please give a clear and concise overview of your proposal. Share any data you have about why you think this is the way forward. Stick to the facts. Person B, please listen but do not interrupt or refute anything*

at this stage. When A is done, I am going to ask you to give a short summary of the key points made by A."

Step 3 – Ask each person to become a champion for what the other person wants: Ask the parties to take turns telling the other party what he or she heard them say was most important. Ask them to show empathy for the other person's needs and interests.

"I'd like you to each tell the other person what you heard them say was most important to them. Then share your take on why they feel that way."

Step 4 – Generate a list of common interests to foster a sense of unity: Ask the parties to identify the parts of each of their separate positions that are common or similar. Ask each of them to identify what they liked about the other person's proposal. Highlight everything that matters equally to both parties. Reconfirm your joint commitment to building shared strategy.

"I'm going to ask you to look at your notes and tell me what you see that's similar in your two solutions. What do you have in common? What did you think was positive about each other's ideas? This is going to help us figure out what matters most to both of you."

Step 5 – Zero in on what's most important for each party: By now you will have a list of what's most important. Start with any common interests that were identified and ratify that these need to be part of the final solution. Then focus on the top one to three things on each of the separate lists.

"We have a list of all the things that you have in common. Now let's sort through the things that you each really want that aren't the same. Each of you tell me what it would take for you to be able to accept what the other person wants that you don't personally favor."

Step 6 – Build an option that includes what matters most to each party: Brainstorm some potential alternatives that incorporate what's important to both parties. Test drive each one without dismissing anything out of hand. Encourage both parties to continue entertaining the new middle-ground solutions until they arrive at that middle place. Keep paraphrasing and encouraging exploration until heads start to nod. Once you've helped them create a compromise position, end by asking each party if they're certain they can live with the final solution.

"I really want to thank you for being so open today and for taking a serious look at what the other person is suggesting. What does it look like when you combine what you have in common and also take into account what's most important to both of you? Is there a plan that gives you each most of what you wanted?"

When compromise is built in a respectful and reciprocal manner, it builds goodwill. This creates trust, which is the essential glue of all relationships. Taking the time to build a *Win/Win compromise* when people are polarized, builds bridges where the traditional method of negotiation burns them.

Technique # 4 – Redirecting Ineffective Behaviors

From time to time those around us behave badly. They might interrupt, say inappropriate things, or fail to keep a commitment. The list of possible ineffective behaviors is endless!

The good news is that there's a safe and nonconfrontational way to respond assertively to people who are being inappropriate. Facilitators use this technique in meetings in order to correct poor behaviors without causing offence. It is equally useful in one-on-one settings.

The Formula for Redirecting Behavior

1. **Describe the ineffective behavior** to raise awareness:

   "I see that…." or *"I'm noticing that…."*

2. **Describe the impact** as a concern for that person:

   "I'm concerned that …"

3. **Offer specific instructions** about what you need them to do:

   "I need you to..." or *" Would you please…."*

Statement # 1 is designed to raise people's awareness about their behavior, i.e. that they were shouting, sounding sarcastic, interrupting, etc.

Statement # 2 signals that you're acting in the person's best interest.

Statement # 3 clearly describes what you need the other person to do.
Look for examples of intervention statements on pages 56 and 57.

Examples of Intervention Language

When two people are side chatting:

> *"Alan. Sue. I see you having a discussion. I'm concerned that we're no longer getting the benefit of your ideas. Please, we need you back."*

When one person dominates the discussion:

> *"Joe, I'm noticing that you've already shared a lot of ideas. I'm concerned that you're not going to get to hear anyone else's report. Please wrap up with a summary of the most important ideas that you've shared so far."*

When two people are arguing and not listening to each other:

> *"I'm noticing that you're each repeating your points. I'm concerned that you may not be hearing each other's ideas. Let's start over, only this time tell us what you think the other person is saying."*

When members are disregarding their own norms:

> *"I'm noticing that you're ignoring some of your own rules. So let's stop and look at the norms we set. What do we need to do to ensure they're being followed?"*

When the meeting has totally digressed:

> *"I'd like to point out that you're now discussing a topic that isn't on the agenda. I'm concerned that we aren't going to get to end on time. Do you want to continue discussing this topic, or should we park it?"*

When someone is being sarcastic:

> *"Ellen, I'm concerned that your ideas aren't being heard because of the tone of voice you're using. Please make your point again, only in a more neutral way."*

When one person is putting down the ideas of another:

> *"Joe, you've been listing the cons of Carol's ideas. I'm concerned that we haven't tapped into your expertise. Please tell Carol what you think is good about her idea and offer her some suggestions that she can use."*

When someone has hurled a personal slur at someone else:

> *"Jim, rather than characterizing Sally as being sloppy, please tell her specifically what you need her to do differently."*

When the meeting has stalled:

> *"I'm noticing that I haven't written anything for a while. I'm concerned the meeting may be stalled. What can we do to get things going again?"*

When the whole group looks exhausted:

> *"I'm noticing that people are slumped in their seats and that we're not making much progress. Tell me what this means and what we should do about it."*

Norm-based Interventions

One of the advantages of creating a set of behavioral norms is that these can be used to leverage ineffective behaviors. When group members break one of the rules that they set themselves, their norms can be used as the basis for the intervention. Here are some examples:

When people run in and out:

> *"I'm noticing that several people have left the meeting this hour. I'm concerned that you're breaking a rule you set earlier. Please remember your commitment not to come and go during the meeting."*

When people talk over each other:

> *"I'm concerned that you're breaking your own rule about only one conversation at a time. Please remember that you agreed to listen actively while others are speaking."*

When people get out their laptops and handhelds:

> *"I'm noticing that several people are texting. I'm concerned that you're ignoring the rule you set earlier about this. Please hold off until the break."*

When a team member interrupts:

> *"Please remember our rule about letting people finish their thoughts."*

You may have noticed that there's no name-calling or aggressive language when using this technique. Instead, factual and straightforward language is used. You may also have noticed that each example provided very specific details about the behavior that's needed. This future orientation helps people move toward a more effective way of interacting.

Redirecting behavior is not aggressive since it's never done to call someone out, make them look bad or put them in their place. It is, nonetheless, assertive and sends the message that you're not going to let ineffective behavior derail the team.

Technique # 5 – Dealing With Resistance

It's understandable that change generates resistance. Generally speaking, people start to resist when they think that a change will bring about negative consequences. This resistance can be out in the open, although it often stays hidden as simple noncompliance. Whenever you encounter resistance, the following technique will provide you with a simple set of steps for dealing with it, whether you're with a group or just talking to one person.

It's important to note that there's a right and a wrong way to deal with resistance. Using the wrong way will make the resistance grow. People may appear to give in, but at a gut level their buy-in will be low and their engagement will be half-hearted. Choosing the wrong approach makes it a battle of wills. Choosing the right approach changes the dialogue into one of mutual problem solving.

The worst way to handling resistance:

Announce the change. Defend it against all objections. Argue back. Sell the change. Try to prove you're right. Use whatever power you've got to force people to capitulate. Cajole, chide, even beg. When that fails to work, tell people that they have no choice.

The ineffectiveness of this directive approach for managing resistance stems from the use of force. They push back, so you push back too, causing them to either go underground or push back even harder. The net effect of relying on compliance is a total lack of buy-in. When people lack buy-in, they don't make an effort.

There's a better way to respond to resistance that makes use of facilitation tools and techniques. This approach lets people talk about their concerns, then engages them in identifying strategies to overcome those fears. At the end of this approach, people feel that they've been heard and that they helped create a solution. This increases their sense of engagement. Here are the steps in the process:

Step #1: Vent their concerns: Invite resistors to describe their reasons for disliking the change proposal. Do not refute their points, defend or cajole. Listen actively, stay neutral and paraphrase key points, even if you don't agree with them. No matter what they say, or how they say it, remain calm and act totally supportive of the resistors. Make them feel they can let it all out. Keep paraphrasing their words back to them. End with a summary of their issues. Show empathy.

Say things like:
> *"Tell me why you're not keen on doing this."*
> *"What are you worried is going to happen?"*
> *"What consequences do you think this will have for you?"*
> *"So you're saying that............"*
> *"I totally understand how you feel."*
> *"Thank you for being open and confiding your feelings."*

Then ask what's known as the transition question: *"Can I ask you a question?"*

If they say "No," this means they haven't finished venting. Go back to Step 1. If they say "Yes," proceed to Step 2.

Step #2: Resolving blocks and barriers: After all the concerns have been expressed and acknowledged, ask the resistors questions that prompt them to suggest solutions to the barriers. This questioning is intentionally detailed and complex so that the resistors have to think deeply about possible ways to move forward. Ask questions like:

"What would you have to believe was true about the change to be open to considering it?"
"What help or support would you need to consider giving it a try?"
"What further information or assurances do you need?"
"What can I do to make this work for you?"

When resistors respond to these questions, they're basically working out their own resistance. If you apply this technique correctly, the resistors should do most of the talking. Your role is to support them while they deal with the barriers themselves.

Why This Approach Works

Taking the two-step questioning approach works because resistors are allowed to vent their frustrations. Then resistors are consulted about what to do next. Since people don't generally refuse to act on their own suggestions, most people will abandon their resistance and move forward.

Refer to page 111 to see an agenda aimed at overcoming resistance to change. This agenda is an adaptation of these principles for use with a large group.

Technique # 6 - Mediating a Dispute

Consultants who are managing lengthy projects commonly encounter situations in which two people become embroiled in a conflict and are no longer on speaking terms. Sometimes these disputes blow over. There are times, however, when the issue and related hard feelings don't fade away on their own. In these instances, the parties need to be brought together to settle their differences.

The big mistake that people make when discussing a dispute is that they focus on dredging up the past. The more they talk about who said or did what, the angrier they become. The other common mistake is that both parties in the dispute talk at the same time. Before long, no one's listening and the dialogue turns into an argument. These pitfalls can all be avoided by using a process called *Needs and Offers Dialogue.*

The technique of *Needs and Offers Dialogue* is a constructive conversation between two parties in a dispute. Its purpose is to vent concerns and resolve interpersonal issues in a low-risk manner so that positive relations can be restored.

Needs and Offers Dialogue can be facilitated in a group setting between two teams or it can be used one-to-one. First we will outline the steps and rules of this process when it is used by a neutral third party who's helping two individuals who are embroiled in a dispute.

Step #1: Approach the parties in the dispute individually to discuss their participation in the dialogue. Explain the goal of the exercise and the rules. Gain the buy-in of the parties. If you encounter resistance, refer to the technique for overcoming resistance on page 58.

Step #2: Find a private place for the meeting. Set a positive tone at the outset by talking about the value of giving and receiving feedback.

Step #3: Introduce the rules of the dialogue and describe the steps. Write the rules shown below on a flip chart or whiteboard for all to see.

The rules for today's discussion:

- Approach the exercise with the positive intention of ending the dispute.
- Anything said in the room stays in the room.
- No one will raise their voice or display anger or frustration.
- Maintain neutral body language: no eye rolling or sighing.
- Never interrupt while the other person has the floor.
- Listen to the views of the other party and make notes.
- Play back to the other person what they're saying.
- Be willing to make changes to improve relations.
- Follow through on the commitments made in the session.

Step #4: Invite each person to make a brief statement about what they would gain if the dispute were to be resolved.

Step #5: Flip a coin to determine who will speak first. That person will tell the other party his side of the story. This must be a factual retelling of the events that occurred and the impact on him. He is not allowed to attribute motives to the other person or indulge in name calling or making negative generalizations. Also insist that the parties speak to each other and not to you.

While the first person is speaking, the other person must maintain eye contact and use body language that is both respectful and nonjudgmental. She must also make notes about what the other person is saying even if he totally disagrees with their views. If either party interrupts, or starts to behave in an inappropriate manner, immediately stop them and redirect their behavior. Refer to page 56 for wording.

Step # 6: Once the first person has given his version of events, the listener reads back her notes. If the first speaker is satisfied that his views have been accurately understood, repeat Step 5 with the second speaker.

Step #7: End the face-to-face session. Send the two parties to separate rooms or at least the far corners of the same room for about 25 to 30 minutes. During this time, they are to write out a list of the specific things they need from each other in order to put the dispute behind them. Encourage them to make reasonable requests and to avoid language that sounds judgmental. Such language will only inflame the dispute.

Step #8: When both parties have written their lists of needs, bring them back together. Ask the first person to read his list of needs. While that party is sharing his needs, the other person must listen actively, then provide a summary of the things that have been requested. The listener can ask questions of clarification but may not refute anything being requested or argue back. Repeat this step with the second person.

Step #9: Once both people have heard each other's needs, have them exchange notes. Then separate them again for another period of 25 to 30 minutes during which time each person will write out a list of offers that respond to the other person's needs.

Step #10: Bring the parties back together to take turns reading their offers aloud. Allow for clarification. Ask each person if the offers are sufficient to resolve the issue. If both parties indicate that they're satisfied with the other person's offer, move to the next step.

If one or both parties indicate that the offers are not adequate for resolving the dispute, invite the dissatisfied party to restate his needs and the other party to amend their offers. Do this until both parties are satisfied that they've heard offers that will end the dispute.

Step #11: Establish a follow-up mechanism. It's customary to set a date to bring both parties back to determine whether their dispute has been resolved. Collect both pages of offers and have them typed and distributed to the parties.

Refer to page 108 for a step-by-step set of process notes for a version of this dialogue between yourself and your client.

Technique # 7 – Giving and Receiving Feedback

Feedback is the process of providing information about past performance with the positive goal of helping individuals improve. Being able to give feedback is critically important to anyone working with a team.

The principles of effective feedback

Feedback is always meant to be constructive: it's never done to criticize or offend. Regardless of the situation, these general principles always apply:

- **Check the facts** - Ensure your understanding is accurate and fair. Investigate actual events to avoid misjudging the situation.
- **Time it** – Offer the feedback as soon as possible after the situation to be discussed.
- **Find a private space** - Hold the feedback session somewhere that's both private and free from distractions.
- **Be personally present** - Don't speak from behind a desk or stand at a distance. Sit close to the person, make eye contact, be attentive to what the other person is saying.
- **Demonstrate caring** - Use language that conveys your positive intention to be helpful and supportive.
- **Be descriptive rather than evaluative** - Tell the other person what you've noticed or what has happened. Avoid any judgmental comments or personal labels.
- **Be specific instead of general** - Describe exactly what happened, so that facts, not impressions, form the basis of the feedback.
- **Focus on what can be changed** - Make suggestions for improvements that the person is capable of implementing.
- **Be systematic** - Follow the eight-step feedback process.

The Eight-Step Feedback Process

Step 1: Ask Permission to Offer Feedback.

State your interest in sharing feedback. If other people resist taking part in a feedback session, refer to the technique for overcoming resistance described earlier in this chapter.

> *"I'd like to share some insights and ideas that I think will be helpful.*
> *Would that be okay?"*

Step 2: Specifically Describe What Happened.

Have your facts lined up. Give a clear and specific description of what has happened. Use objective-sounding language. Avoid generalizing, exaggerating or offering emotional accounts.

> *"During last month's open house, three of the utility crews that you were*

responsible for coordinating did not perform the functions specified in their contracts. Two were late and one did not have the equipment that they needed. When asked why they were so disorganized, they gave me these emails which showed that they had been either given the wrong information or had not been provided with all of the details they should have received."

Step 3: Explain the Direct Impact of the Individual's Actions.

Describe the impact on individuals, the program or the department. Keep it very objective and don't get personal. Avoid blaming. Deal with the facts of the current situation.

> *"Since the utility crews all started to set up late, the entire open house event had to be delayed. The team had to scramble to set up a hosting area at the hotel so that the customers would have somewhere to go while the displays were being assembled. This caused us to have to apologize to our customers and reduced the time of the open house by two full hours."*

Step 4: Give the Person Receiving the Feedback the Opportunity to Explain.

Invite the person receiving the feedback to share his perspective on what transpired. Listen actively, using attentive body language and paraphrasing key points even if you don't agree with their version of events, to demonstrate that you're listening.

> *"Please tell me what happened from your perspective."*

Step 5: Draw Ideas out of the Other Person.

Frame the dialogue as an opportunity to make improvements. Give the other person the opportunity to propose solutions before you offer your ideas. This will allow you to gauge how much self-awareness they have about the situation.

> *"What do you suggest so that this kind of thing never happens again?"*

Step 6: Offer Specific Suggestions for Improvement.

Make suggestions that will improve the situation. Wherever possible, build on the ideas that the other person has already put forward.

> *"I like your idea that you keep a master checklist of all the things that you'll do one day before each event and also the day of each event. In addition, I suggest that you get each of the utilities contractors to call you the day before an event to have a verbal review of all the details, just to close any gaps."*

Step 7: Summarize and Express Your Support.

Demoralizing people never sets the stage for improved performance, so it's important to offer encouragement and end on an optimistic note.

"I want to thank you for being so open and for offering improvement ideas. I'm confident that you will do a great job at the next event!"

Step 8: Follow Up

Feedback is only effective if it actually leads to change. Be sure to end the feedback session with clear action steps. This ensures that the whole exercise doesn't need to be repeated.

"I'm going to check with you about a week before the next open house to see if you feel your systems are working and to see if you need any assistance either from myself or from someone else on the team."

Receiving Feedback With Grace

Feedback is a two-way street: sometimes we're on the receiving end. If you sense that your client is unhappy with your performance, it's important to address those concerns quickly. It's a core facilitator value to invite clients to give specific feedback in the middle and at the end of every engagement. Since it's hard for people to give feedback, it's important to say and do things that make it easier for them. Here are some guidelines about what to do when you're on the receiving end of feedback:

- **Be open and accepting** - Even if you don't relish the idea of receiving feedback, act like you're fine with it.

    "I'm very open to hearing how I can improve."

- **Try to avoid becoming emotional** - Breathe deeply. Sit back. Adopt a relaxed body posture. Lower your voice. Speak slowly.

    "Tell me what you think I'm currently doing that's not working."

- **Listen actively** - Make eye contact with the speaker. Paraphrase what they're saying even if you don't agree.

    "So you're saying that I don't return emails or phone calls promptly."

- **Ask Questions** - Ask follow-on questions to get more details about their perspective on the situation.

    "Can you describe some recent examples?"

- **Don't get defensive** - Understand the other person's perspective before presenting your side of the story. Ask for more details.

  "I'm aware that I don't look at email often enough, but I thought I was on top of my phone calls. What do you suggest would be a better way to manage my calls?"

- **Offer solutions** - Don't wait to be told what you could do, instead offer up suggestions. Make sure it responds to at least some of what the client wants or they'll feel that you're ignoring their feelings and needs.

  "I'm thinking that I need to route all of my calls to my home office so that the staff can ask each caller when they need to hear back. Then, I can set my phone on vibrate so that my office can give me a heads up about an urgent call even when I'm in a meeting."

- **Thank the person who gave you the feedback** - Unless the feedback session was cruel or conducted with negative intentions, extend thanks to the person who took the time to talk to you.

  "I really appreciate that you took the time to tell me what's been bothering you. I don't want you to ever hold back if you have something I should know about."

- **Work to improve** - If you acknowledge feedback and then ignore it, the relationship with the other person will worsen. In the workplace, feedback sessions are often a last chance to improve.

  "You're going to notice improved communication from me in the future. In fact, I'll check in with you in two weeks to see if you've seen any improvement."

- **Follow up** - Periodically let those who gave you the feedback know what you're doing in response to their input.

  "Have I been doing any better at communicating lately?"

Chapter Five – Facilitating Effective Meetings

Meetings are an essential business tool. They represent important opportunities to share information, plan strategies, build relationships and jointly solve problems. Unfortunately, too many meetings waste valuable time and energy. Anyone who attends a lot of meetings has experienced the main pitfalls:

- an insufficiently detailed agenda
- the absence of key people
- poor time management
- the tendency to get side-tracked and go off topic
- rehashing the same topic over and over
- lack of closure and insufficiently detailed action plans
- failure to bring forward past action items

Added to these problems are common behavioral dysfunctions like lack of real listening, people talking over each other and emotional arguing. Technology has further undermined meetings as people now check messages during discussions.

The Traits of All Truly Effective Meetings
<ul><li>There's a detailed agenda that's sent out ahead of time so that participants can prepare.</li><li>The meeting participants have agreed to abide by a set of norms or meeting guidelines.</li><li>There's a clear framework for each topic. This includes the name of the agenda item, the expected outcome or purpose of the discussion, a short description of the process to be used and the timeframe for each topic.</li><li>There's a clear indication of who needs to take part in each agenda item. This allows people to leave meetings when they're not needed.</li><li>Whenever possible, information sharing and updates are posted on the intranet or shared via emails to save valuable meeting time.</li><li>The person leading the meeting knows how to intervene to park off-topic items, refocus a rambling conversation and make sure that everyone is heard.</li><li>All decision-making conversations are structured using process tools. The process tool or approach to be used is described at the start of each discussion.</li><li>Feedback about meeting quality is sought on a bi-monthly basis using a simple *Pluses and Deltas* format. On an annual basis, a more detailed meeting effectiveness survey is conducted for each group that meets on a regular basis. This survey is followed up with a discussion to identify ways to make meetings better.</li></ul>

Meeting Best Practices

Ensure productive meetings by implementing these simple tools and practices:

Pre-meeting:

- Use emails and mechanisms like surveys as an alternative to meetings wherever possible to reduce the amount of face-to-face time needed.
- Identify who needs to attend which portions of the meeting and invite only those who are essential.
- Circulate a detailed agenda that describes the objectives and the times for each topic so that participants can prepare.

To Start:

- Begin with a review of the topics and the expected outcomes for each.
- Reiterate the meeting guidelines and ask if any additional rules are needed for that meeting.
- Ask someone to help you manage the time or set up an automatic timer.
- Set up a *Parking Lot* sheet of paper and explain that you will use it to capture all topics that are best addressed at another time.
- Before starting each new topic, identify the nature of the discussion. Is it to share information, plan strategy, solve a problem or build relationships?
- Start each discussion by clarifying the purpose of the conversation, the expected outcomes, the process to be used and the timeframe.
- For each new agenda item, also clarify whether the group members are empowered to make the decision or are simply being asked for their input for a decision that will be made elsewhere.
- Regardless of whether or not you will be neutral during a specific discussion, make accurate notes on a flip chart to capture client ideas.

During Discussions:

- Monitor time and tactfully point out time milestones.
- Point out any off-topic items and ask permission to place them into the *Parking Lot.*
- Keep track of who is speaking and call on quiet people.
- Ping-pong ideas around to ensure that there's conversation between group members.
- Conduct periodic process checks. Ask people if they feel progress is being made, if the process seems to be working, if the pace seems right and how they are feeling.
- Summarize periodically, especially during complicated discussions, to make sure that key ideas are being fully understood and to refocus attention.

To Wrap Up:

- Start to wrap up ten minutes before the scheduled end of the meeting.
- Give clear summaries of all the main points shared at the meeting, especially the decisions that were made.
- Review all action plans. Include a description of what completion looks like, responsibilities and due dates.
- Schedule the next meeting.
- Invite people to provide feedback as they exit the meeting.

Meeting Guidelines or Behavioral Norms

Any meeting can be improved by inviting the participants to suggest behavioral norms. Norms are rules that everyone agrees to abide by. Since this is a technical sounding term, norms are generally referred to as meeting guidelines. They are also sometimes called a code of conduct.

Norms, or meeting guidelines, are the rules that the members of a group agree to follow. Below are examples of common group norms. You can suggest these to a new group and ask folks to ratify them, but remember that norms are more likely to be effective if you allow them to come from group members.

If you can't picture yourself having this discussion with a room full of people, you can ask people to suggest meeting guidelines during your one-on-one interviews with them. You can also send out an email inviting people to suggest meeting guidelines. Just tabulate the suggestions, then feed them back to the group at a meeting. Ask folks to ratify the rules. Once you have a set of rules, circulate them and/or post them in the meeting room as a reminder.

Since circumstances change all the time, new rules will be needed from time to time. One way to generate new norms is to ask for suggestions anytime there's an issue. Below are some of the norms groups commonly set:

- We will listen actively and not interrupt when others are speaking.
- We will each ensure that we don't personally dominate any meeting by monitoring our own participation.
- We will speak openly and honestly during meetings, then keep all confidential information private.
- When we encounter differing points of view, we will debate the facts of the situation without personal enmity.
- Any personal feedback to a colleague must be constructive.
- We will each honor meeting start and end times.
- We will each make an effort to stay on track and on time within the agenda time limits.
- We will each avoid actions that disrupt the meeting like side-chatting or walking in and out.
- Anyone can call a time out if they need a break.
- We will all avoid nonessential texting and emailing during meetings.
- We will put away laptops and cell phones anytime a colleague indicates that an agenda item requires everyone's full attention.
- We will each contribute our ideas and resources to the team and also share the responsibility for the work of the team.

Examples of the kinds of questions to ask when setting norms can be found on pages 32 and 49.

The All-Important Status Update Meetings

Section Two of this book features detailed step-by-step facilitator notes about how to conduct a wide variety of idea-generation and decision-making meetings. Most of these meetings are typically held only once during the lifespan of a typical project. The type of meeting that takes place most often in projects is the *Status Update Meeting*. These meetings happen anywhere from once a month to several times a week.

Status Update Meetings are about exchanging information: just presentations and current project status. They're designed purely to make sure that everyone's in the loop. They're not designed to generate a lot of discussion. That's what helps keep them short and crisp. This parameter needs to be stated explicitly at the beginning of each of these meetings so that everyone is clear about the scope. Issues or differing points of view should be noted and taken off-line for further discussion at a well-structured decision-making meeting like the ones in the next section. While *Status Update Meeting* formats vary, most include the following standard items:

The Status-Update Meeting Format *

- <u>Roll call</u>. Invite meeting participants to share their names, the areas they represent and their role in the project.
- <u>Accomplishments.</u> Ask everyone, in turn, to list their most recent developments and successes. Record these in the minutes.
- <u>The status of work.</u> Go around the group to hear updates on progress as compared to what was originally planned, unexpected wins and issues that others should be aware of.
- <u>Work scheduled but not complete.</u> Review any items on the work plan that were scheduled to be completed but have not been started or are behind schedule. Explore the reasons for any delays and commit to new target dates.
- <u>Project Issues.</u> Identify any ongoing issues affecting the project that could impact progress and have not been resolved. Identify who needs to work on which specific problems.
- <u>Imminent actions.</u> Ask each team member to offer a quick snapshot of what they're doing next and anything they need from other members of the team to support their action.

---

*Adapted from *The Project Meeting Facilitator* by Tammy Adams and Jan Means.

See a step-by-step description of a Status-Update Meeting on page 94.

Evaluate Meetings Regularly

Teams that meet on a regular basis should consider conducting a *Pluses and Deltas* process once every three or four months. The following are the very simple steps in this valuable activity:

- At the start of the meeting, post a sheet of flip-chart paper with two columns: one for pluses and one for deltas. The pluses side is for collecting sticky notes about what worked well at the meeting. The deltas side of the page is for collecting sticky notes that describe suggestions for improving future meetings.
- Hand out sticky note pads in two colors so that group members can record what they like about the group's meetings on one color and their improvement suggestions on another color.
- As members leave the session they simply post their sticky notes on the *Pluses and Deltas* pages.
- Ask a team member to volunteer to read and sort the notes to eliminate duplicates.
- The chart is brought back at the start of the next meeting so that members can discuss and ratify the improvement suggestions in the deltas column.

Deltas will result in either action steps or new norms. The new norms can be added to the existing list of meeting guidelines. Improvements can be implemented immediately. Repeating this activity a few times a year will incrementally improve meeting efficiency and member satisfaction.

Conduct An Annual Meeting Survey

During a long project that involves a lot of meeting time, it's advisable to send out a short survey. This allows people to vent any negative feelings that they might have regarding project meetings. It also lets you turn dissatisfaction with meetings into improvement ideas.

The annual meeting survey can be completed and tallied online. Use the questions on the next page as possible survey items. Bring the results to a team meeting and facilitate the structured conversation outlined in detail on page 106.

Meeting Survey Components

Rate the meetings held by our project team based on the following indicators. All ratings are anonymous and will be feedback to team members in tabulated form.

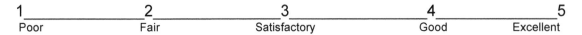

1	2	3	4	5
Poor	Fair	Satisfactory	Good	Excellent

Agenda: Are agendas clear and detailed enough to provide a good framework?

Preparation: How well do people do their homework and come prepared?

Active Listening: How good are we at listening attentively to each other?

Participation: Rate the extent to which everyone gets heard at meetings.

Differing Views: How good are we at objectively debating the facts of a situation rather than getting caught up in emotional arguing?

Process: How good are we at structuring decision-making conversations?

Focus: How good are we about staying on topic and not wandering?

Meeting Times: How good are we at starting and ending on time?

Time Management: How good are we at staying within the time limits as set out in the agenda?

Productivity: How effective are we at getting things done and leaving meetings with concrete action steps?

Attention: How good are we at turning off laptops and handhelds during important discussions?

Quality of Decision Making: Rate the extent to which we make high quality decisions as a team.

Amount of Time Spent in Meetings: Rate the appropriateness of the total number of hours this team spends in meetings on a monthly basis.

Face-to-Face or Virtual?

Today, more and more meetings are taking place via the Internet and conference calls. This saves time and connects people who are geographically dispersed, but generally tends to make meetings worse since it's much harder to instill teamwork and have deep discussions when people can't see each other.

Despite the fact that face-to-face meetings are better than virtual ones, the effectiveness of both meeting types can be greatly improved if they're properly structured. In the second section of this book, you will find structured processes that can be conducted both in person or at a distance.

Surveys can be handed out and tabulated manually or sent out via email and tabulated online. Problems can be analyzed at a meeting or via the Internet. In every instance, meetings are better when properly structured.

Part 2 – Structured Conversations

During every consulting assignment, there are key conversations that you need to be able to facilitate. This section of the book outlines those discussions in step-by-step detail, so that you have a clear game plan.

Nothing is worse than running an important decision-making session without structure. This is especially true when key stakeholders are present. Lack of structure allows the conversations to veer off track. It also emboldens talkative people to take over and make all the decisions. In contrast, having a well-designed set of steps will make you look both prepared and in control.

The agendas in this section of the book:

- describe the essential conversations that every consultant needs to know how to facilitate
- provide clear, step-by-step guidance, including tools for making group decisions
- ensure that all voices are heard and that there's buy-in to the outcome

Each conversation in this section of the book is described as if you were meeting people both face-to-face and virtually. Having everyone in the same room is always the best way to meet, since personal contact builds relationships and encourages true collaboration. Having said that, we live in a global business environment where more and more meetings are conducted at a distance. In keeping with that reality, each set of meeting design notes also describes the steps to take in order to conduct that meeting virtually.

Note that the agendas that follow have timeframes associated with each discussion. These times are purely speculative and are based on estimates of how long each conversation typically takes given the number of estimated participants. You will, of course, need to adjust these times to accommodate the number of individuals actually in attendance.

The best way to take advantage of this section of the book is to read through the conversations to understand how they're structured. Then use this section the way you would use a cookbook: follow each set of instructions closely at least once. Later you'll be able to improvise to make them your own.

Supplies You Will Need

Flip-chart stands and paper

If you're facilitating a face-to-face meeting, you will either need to acquire a flip-chart stand with a large paper pad or find a room with a whiteboard. This will allow you to make notes while each discussion unfolds. Some of the conversations require the use of more than one flip-chart stand. If the room has large empty walls, you can sometimes skip the stands and stick the flip-chart paper directly onto the walls.

Tape

Unless you're using self-stick flip-chart paper, you will need a roll of blue painter's tape that doesn't damage walls or leave a sticky residue.

Markers

Buy only chisel-tip markers, not the pointy ones. People also appreciate the nontoxic kind because they don't emit fumes and stains come out in the wash.

Stick-on Voting Dots

To conduct multi-voting activities, purchase sticky dots at a stationary store. These dots are made for marking file folders in medical offices. The dots come on sheets. Before your meeting, cut the sheets into strips so that they're ready to be handed out when you need them.

A *Parking Lot* Sheet

At every meeting, tape a flip-chart sheet to a side wall. Write the words *Parking Lot* at the top of the page. If any conversation goes off track, point out the digression and ask the group if they need to continue the discussion or if the off-track item ought to be added to a future agenda. At the end of each meeting, review the items in the *Parking Lot* to identify if and when they need to be addressed.

A Smart Phone or Tablet

You can skip the chore of dragging unwieldy flip-chart paper away from meetings by simply taking photos of the notes. This also lets you instantly share meeting highlights. To help maximize precious meeting time, download a free timer app. The best displays are those that feature a countdown clock like one named *Giant Timer*. Display the countdown to make everyone aware that time is marching along and to encourage people to stay on task.

Software

For virtual meetings, you will need to find a software program that allows meeting participants to see the notes you're making as the discussion unfolds. You will also need to acquire and learn how to deploy software that tabulates survey results and adds the results of multi-votes.

The Structured Conversations

Structured Conversation # 1 - Discovery

Specifications: Nothing is more important than truly understanding your clients: their history, their goals, their challenges and their management philosophy. Discovery is typically done through research and one-on-one interviews. (See the discovery questions on page 29.) Even if you do background research and conduct one-on-one interviews, it may be a good idea to also have a discovery conversation with a group of stakeholders.

When discovery is conducted in a group setting, people are stimulated by the comments of their colleagues. This results in a more detailed and nuanced profile of the organization. Note that this meeting is non-decision-making in nature, since the goal is to gather information. That means that while you can take the pulse of the group to determine the extent to which people share the same views, there is no need to reach a consensus. This meeting is designed to help you understand the organization more than create a vision or set objectives for the consulting assignment. The ideal group size for this conversation is eight to twelve participants.

Purpose: To engage key stakeholders in a discovery conversation to
build a picture of the organization's history and culture.

Agenda	Process Design Notes
Welcome (5 minutes)	• Describe the purpose of the meeting. • Review the meeting agenda.
Sequential Questioning (60 minutes)	• Ask group members to write their names on slips of paper. Collect the slips and place them in a pile in front of you. Explain that you will be presenting a series of statements and then selecting one person to respond to each one. • Before this meeting you will have written the selected questions/statements on a pad of flip-chart paper. Write one question or statement at the top of each sheet, leaving room to record comments. Remind people that only the person whose name is drawn gets to respond. • Flip the sheet and read the first question/statement. Pause to allow time for reflection. Call out the first name. Allow that person to answer. Ask probing questions. Record the person's key points, then open the floor to anyone else who wants to add their thoughts. • Repeat this process for each question until everyone has been called on to respond at least once. You can go around more than once if you have a small group. Remember to read back a summary of your notes for each question before moving to the next question. • The following questions/statements are suggested. You can,

of course, pose other questions. Most should be open-ended, but a few closed-ended questions should always be included since they stimulate a definitive response.

- *"What has been the most outstanding achievement of the organization, and what conditions made it possible?"*
- *"If I were to interview your most satisfied customers, what would they say about your products/services?"*
- *"If I were to interview your competitors, what do you think they would tell me was the thing that scares them most about you?"*
- *"Rate the current organizational state on a scale of 1 -10, in which 10 is perfection. Explain your rating."*
- *"If you could turn back the hands of time, what one event would you go back and change?"*
- *"Our organization is horizontally integrated. We are not trapped in silos: true or false?"*
- *"Our organization is very adaptable and responsive to change: true or false?"*
- *"Our upper management group regularly seeks out employee input on matters that affect the organization: true or false?"*
- *"Is there anything about your organization that an outsider would find remarkable or surprising?"*

Closing
(10 minutes)

- Go around the group and ask each person to share at least one major insight that they gained from the discovery discussion.
- Discuss whether the information from this conversation should/will be shared. Decide on how to communicate the information.

Adjourn

If this is a virtual conversation:

- o List the names of the meeting participants.
- o During a videoconference or group call, read one question at a time.
- o Call on one person to respond to each question or statement.
- o Ask the responder follow-on questions.
- o Invite others to also answer the question. Keep track of who has spoken so no one is missed. Record comments and offer a summary of each question before moving on.
- o Clarify with the group whether or not they wish to receive a summary.
- o Adjourn.

Structured Conversation # 2 - Environmental Scanning

Specifications: In most projects, the parameters are clearly defined before the consultant is hired. Despite the fact that the basic outline of the project is in place, you may find it advantageous to hold strategy discussions to build participation and buy-in for your project. This meeting is an ideal activity for the key stakeholders or the new project team.

This first aspect of strategy planning engages the client in looking around to ensure that nothing of significance has been missed. This meeting works best when there are from eight to twenty participants. If the group has fewer members, run it without breaking into subgroups. This will make the meeting shorter.

In this section of the book, strategy development is divided into two separate meetings. This one focuses on scanning the environment. The second part is outlined in Conversation # 4 - Vision and Mission. Breaking these discussions into separate meetings allows you the flexibility of conducting the sessions together or separately.

Purpose: To gain an understanding of the forces at work
in the environment in order to assess their impact and
develop strategies for managing them.

Agenda	Process Design Notes
Welcome (5 minutes)	• Describe the purpose of the meeting. • Review the meeting agenda. • Review and ratify the norms for the meeting. (pg 68)
Introductions (5 minutes)	• Introduce yourself. • Invite others to self-introduce.
SWOT Analysis (45 minutes)	• Set up four flip charts or tape flip-chart paper to the walls in four locations, one for each of the topics below. Invite people to divide themselves evenly between the four topics. Allow groups to stay at each topic for 10 minutes. Have them appoint someone to take notes about their discussion. • Every ten minutes, ask the groups to move to the next topic until everyone has addressed all four sets of questions. (Be sure to ask recorders to write small and not repeat points already mentioned by previous groups.) • Here are the four topics in a SWOT discussion: **Strengths:** What are the outstanding strengths of the organization, of its products/services, of its people, of

its place in the market/community? What's the company's strategic advantage?

Weaknesses: What are the things that we typically don't do well? Where are we weak? What things do we often get wrong? Where do we tend to fall short? What have we never been able to master/accomplish?

Opportunities: What opportunities are staring us in the face right now? What could we achieve if we get ourselves properly positioned? What could this project achieve if we really set a stretch goal?

Threats: What could derail us? What are the hidden dangers that we've missed or ignored? What megatrends are out there?

Plenary Session (10 minutes)	• Ask someone at each board to read the recorded comments to the whole group. Invite questions and comments.
Idea Ranking (10 minutes)	• Give each person four strips of peel-off voting dots. Each strip should have four dots. They can all be the same value or they can be weighted. • Invite people to wander from chart to chart to place their dots on the four items on each page that they personally think are most important.
Idea Consolidation (15 Minutes)	• Ask for volunteers to add up the dots to identify the top-ranked items for each topic. On a new flip-chart sheet, consolidate the top-ranked items by topic.
Strategy Sessions (20 minutes)	• Form small groups of from two to four people. Distribute the top-ranked items to these small groups. • Allow time for each group to identify strategies for dealing with their item. They should identify what needs to be done, how, by whom and by when.
Plenary (30 minutes)	• Bring people together to share strategies. Discuss these with the whole group and ratify the ones that will be implemented. Set a date for reports on progress.
Closing (5 minutes)	• Take pictures of the flip-chart pages for later distribution. • Inform participants when the notes will be distributed. • Invite people to share what they gained from the session.
Adjourn	

If this is a virtual conversation:

- o Send out an email that contains an invitation to take part in a strategy-planning session.
- o Attach a link to a page where people can add their thoughts about strengths, weaknesses, opportunities and threats. Leave this page open for two weeks. People can add their ideas at any time. Ask people to read what others have already written to avoid repeating ideas.
- o Deploy multi-voting software that allows people to select the four most important elements in each category.
- o Send the tabulated results to the group in advance of a conference call so that people can think of solutions.
- o During a videoconference or group call, solicit suggestions for strategies to deal with the top-ranked items in each category. Review all of the suggestions. Hold a verbal multi-vote to identify which strategies should be implemented.
- o Ask for volunteers to develop action plans for the strategies deemed to be most important. Set a time for reporting on the action steps.
- o Adjourn.

Structured Conversation # 3 – Team Launch

Specifications: If your initiative requires a strong team effort, you should hold a meeting that welcomes people and builds a sense of cohesion. This agenda includes basic team-building elements to help team members identify each other's skills and determine how they will work together.

This agenda is short. If time allows, continue the team development process by including Structured Conversation # 4: Vision and Mission, which is another important element in team formation. This meeting agenda assumes a group size of from six to ten participants.

Purpose: To build a foundation for the project team.

Agenda	Process Design Notes
Welcome (3 minutes)	• Describe the purpose of the meeting and review the meeting agenda. • Welcome team members and make a statement about the positive potential of the initiative and how pleased you are to be working with each of them.
Introductions (25 minutes)	• Ask each person to find a partner to interview. Allow about ten minutes for the interviews. On a flip chart or whiteboard, write the topics to be covered in the interviews: name, educational background, role in the organization, proudest professional achievement, skills being brought to the team. • Invite people to introduce their partners to the group. • Introduce yourself at the end.

Team
Norms
(60 minutes)
	• Introduce the idea that teamwork is much more effective when everybody is on the same page about how things get done.
	• Hand out a sheet with four questions and space to write. Allow about three minutes for everyone to complete the questions. The questions are:
	
	  - *"List the things that make meetings a waste of time. What parameters should we put on our meetings so that they avoid these pitfalls and are really effective?"*
	  - *"Describe your idea of effective team communications. What do you need to know, when and what's your preferred way to communicate?"*
	  - *"If we run into problems, how do you want to resolve them? What's your preferred approach to problem*

solving?"
- *"Think back to the best team you ever worked on. What made it great?"*

- Once people have written their comments, facilitate a conversation about each of the questions. This is a decision-making conversation, so you need to bounce ideas around the group before you write them on the flip chart. Read back what you write to make sure that people can live with it. The answers to the first question will give you a set of norms for your meetings. The rest of the questions will give you parameters for how the team will function.

- To continue the team building, proceed to the next conversation about Vision and Mission.

Closing **(5 minutes)**	• Clarify when and how the notes from this meeting will be shared. • Establish the time, place and agenda of the next meeting.
Adjourn	

If this is a virtual conversation:

- ○ Send out an email that contains a short profile of each member of the new team. In that email include the four *Norming* questions mentioned earlier to allow people to prepare.
- ○ Hold a videoconference or group call. Start the call by welcoming everyone and making a positive statement about the strengths of everyone on the team.
- ○ Invite each person to self-introduce using the same headings as mentioned previously. Introduce yourself last.
- ○ Facilitate a discussion based on the four *Norming* questions above. Since this is a decision-making discussion, be sure to encourage people to comment on each other's suggestions. Keep summarizing and ratifying ideas to ensure that everyone can live with the group norms and parameters being set.
- ○ Give a summary of what was discussed. Then inform the group when and where these recommendations will be posted. Stress that this is an iterative process and that new parameters can be added as time goes on. Thank everyone for taking part.
- ○ Adjourn.

Structured Conversation # 4 - Vision and Mission

Specifications: Even when a project has been given a set of parameters, there's real value in bringing the members of the team together to build a shared vision. Think of this as a way to make the parameters come to life and help people make the project their own. This is an ideal team-building activity for the early stage of any team. You could also conduct this session with key stakeholders who are not on the project team but who need to be supportive of your work.

Combine the responses and share them with the participants. After a few months you could bring the details of the Vision back in the form of a survey that lets participants rate the extent to which each item is being achieved. If you use the Vision and Mission as the basis of a survey, refer to the structured conversation on page 106 to process the results.

Purpose: To build a compelling *Vision* for the project and
clarify the mission of the team.

Agenda	Process Design Notes
Welcome (5 minutes)	• Describe the purpose of the meeting. • Review the meeting agenda.
Introductions (20 minutes)	• Ask everyone to pick a partner to interview for six minutes. Have them share their name, role in the organization and hopes and fears related to the initiative. • Ask partners to present each other to the group. • Record the hopes and fears on a flip chart.

Visioning
(45 minutes)
	• Review the original goals and parameters of the project. If you have a handout, share this with the participants. This provides a framework for the *Visioning* exercise.
	• Hand out a single sheet that contains the following *Visioning* questions. Introduce the *Visioning* exercise by asking each person to imagine that this meeting is taking place from one to five years in the future. This might sound something like:
	• *"Imagine that today is not October 10, 2016, but that it's actually October 10, 2018. Our initiative is complete and it's been a HUGE success. It totally surpassed all expectations. Without speaking to anyone, write out your answers to the following questions:"*
	    "What are we celebrating? What's been achieved, improved, created?"
	    "What's noteworthy about the product or service we

created or improved?"

"What have been the effects of the changes that we made on the company's bottom line?"

"How have people been affected by the changes?"

"What was unique about how we went about our work?"

"What did I personally gain from being part of this initiative?"

- Allow about five minutes for people to write out their answers.
- Ask each person to find a partner. Unless people have disabilities, have the partners stand while they exchange views. This adds energy.
- Set a timer for two minutes. Tell people that during this two minutes, only one of the partners is to share what they wrote, while the other person listens. When two minutes are up, announce that it's the second person's turn to talk.
- Set the timer for another two minutes so the second person can talk.
- After both partners have shared their vision, ask everyone to find a new partner. Repeat the process, only shorten the time for the partner sharing to one and a half minutes per turn.
- You can stop here or conduct a third round of partner sharing.
- After these partner dialogues, ask people to return to their seats.

Synthesize
Ideas
(20 minutes)

- Facilitate a discussion to pull together the ideas that the partners shared. Record key ideas on a flip chart or whiteboard. Since this is not meant to be a decision-making conversation, there's no need to have everyone see the same vision.

Mission
Statement
(10 minutes)

- Post the notes so everyone can see them. Hand out colored markers and invite everyone to go up to the flip charts to place a check mark above the three points on each flip-chart sheet that they think are most important. Add up the check marks to identify the areas of greatest concurrence within the group.
- Invite each person to write two to three statements that incorporate elements from the vision for inclusion in a mission statement. These can be sentence fragments.

            Discourage people from trying to craft the perfectly balanced statement since this is very time intensive.

- Invite people to read out what they wrote. There will be repeats. Collect all the statements so that you can work on writing a mission statement that incorporates the key phrases. If there is a talented writer in the group, enlist that person to help.

Closing
(5 minutes)
- Inform the group when and how you will share the draft statement with the group. Thank them for their participation.

Adjourn

If this is a virtual conversation:

- Send out an email explaining the process.
- Send out the *Visioning* questions for each person to complete.
- Ask each person to call two other people working on the initiative to share their visions.
- Open a page online where group members can share their responses to the questions. Allow two weeks for this input phase. Ask people to read what others have written before they add their comments to avoid duplicates.
- Deploy tabulation software that allows group members to multi-vote on which elements they see as most important. Tabulate the results and send an email asking people to review the results.
- Ask people to submit statements that can guide you in writing a mission statement.
- Review the results of the multi-voting exercise during a conference call.
- During a videoconference or group call, read the draft statement to get additional guidance. Ask the group to ratify the final statement.
- Adjourn.

Structured Conversation #5 - Work Planning, Roles and Responsibilities

Specifications: In most major projects, people are assigned roles based on their area of specialty. This is usually done by whoever is managing the project and is then communicated to team members. There are situations, however, when you may need to create a work plan with input from a group. One example of the need to develop a collaborative work plan within a project might be in conjunction with a special event. Let's say your consulting assignment is almost complete and you now need to hold a major exhibit to communicate with a large group of people. If you need to bring a team together to decide who will do what, the following process can be very helpful. It matches people to tasks and ensures that work is fairly distributed. The ideal group size for this conversation is from six to ten participants.

Purpose: To clarify who will be doing what on an
important project activity.

Agenda	Process Design Notes
Welcome (5 minutes)	• Describe the purpose of the meeting. • Review the meeting agenda. • Review and ratify the norms for the meeting. (pg. 68)
Work planning (90 minutes)	• Make sure everyone has information about budget, timeline, expected deliverables of the initiative, etc. • For each objective, ask group members to identify what needs to be done, how and when. Allow time for individual work. You can also pair up team members. • Facilitate a discussion to collect this information. Write a short description of what needs to be done, how and by when for each objective. Leave room under each set of work activities to add more notes. Keep posting the sheets as they fill up. • Lead a thorough discussion of each set of work activities so that team members can comment, share ideas and make changes.
Roles and Responsibilities (60 minutes)	• Help members identify the time, skills and other requirements related to each set of activities. • Introduce criteria that will allow the group to assess the activities as high, medium or low. These criteria are: degree of complexity, degree of difficulty and time required for each. • Begin matching people with activities. Start by allowing people to select their top item. Keep assigning tasks until all items are accounted for. Use the criteria to ensure that no one person has all the difficult tasks while others take on all the simple tasks and those with low time demands.

- Review and ratify the work plan.
- Identify how the work plan will be communicated.

Closing   • Clarify the time, place and agenda of the next meeting.
(5 minutes)

Adjourn

If this is a virtual conversation:

o Send out an email explaining the initiative: Describe objectives, expected deliverables, budgets, timeframes and target audience.
o Create a chart showing each objective. Ask team members to send you detailed information about what needs to be done to achieve each objective, how and when.
o When you've received this information, complete the chart.
o Hold a videoconference or group call to review the chart to ensure that it's accurate and complete.
o Help members identify the time, skills and other requirements related to each set of activities.
o Introduce criteria that will allow the group to assess the activities as high, medium or low. These criteria are: degree of complexity, degree of difficulty and time required for each.
o Ask for input from the group about how they would rate each of the work activities according to the criteria. Listen to all the input but for the sake of simplicity, reserve the right to make the final call on how each activity is rated. At the end of this discussion, you should have some idea about which tasks are complex and time-consuming, compared to those that are simple and quick to complete.
o Begin matching people with activities. Start by allowing people to select their top item. Keep assigning tasks until all tasks have been assigned. Use the criteria to ensure that no one person has all the difficult tasks, while others take on all the simple, quick tasks.
o Adjourn.

Structured Conversation #6 - Risk Assessment

Specifications: Almost all projects encounter circumstances and events that have the potential to hinder progress. While it's impossible to accurately identify every potential risk, it's prudent to think ahead to the most likely problems and develop strategies in case they occur.

This is a decision-making conversation that makes use of a decision grid to help sort risks. Be prepared for lively debates about where each risk ought to be placed within the grid. If possible, avoid playing the role of decision maker. Instead, encourage people to really hear each other, and then help them to find a middle ground.

Write risks on sticky notes so that you can move them around on the grid, since people's understanding of each risk might shift during the discussion. This meeting works best when you include people from outside the project team. This ensures that important risks aren't missed. An alternate approach is to hold the meeting with only the project team, but then circulate the results to key stakeholders for their comments. The timeframes shown below assume a group of ten to fifteen participants.

Purpose: To assess potential risks to the project and
develop contingency plans.

Agenda	Process Design Notes
Welcome (5 minutes)	<ul><li>Describe the purpose of the meeting.</li><li>Review the meeting agenda.</li><li>Review and ratify the norms for the meeting. (pg. 68)</li></ul>
Identify Risks (45 minutes)	<ul><li>Hand out the questions below. Leave room for people to make notes. Allow a few minutes while people think.</li></ul>

- What crises or sudden changes could disrupt the project?
- What assumptions are we currently making that could turn out to be false or slightly off?
- What happens if costs are excessive?
- What could cause timeline slippage?
- What if key people leave the organization?
- How might markets or competitors impact our plans?
- Who or what else might impede our plans?

- Hold a discussion for each question. Encourage people to explore each risk in depth.
- Record them on a flip chart or white board, eliminating all duplicates.

Sort Potential
Risks
(45 minutes)

- Draw the Probability/Impact Grid on a flip chart or whiteboard.

IMPACT → HI	3. Low Probability/ High Impact	1. High Probability/ High Impact
LO ←	4. Low Probability/ Low Impact	2. Hi Probability/ Low Impact

LO ← PROBABILITY → HI

1. High probability/High impact
2. High probability/Low impact
3. Low probability/High impact
4. Low probability/Low impact

- Facilitate a discussion to sort the potential risks into the four boxes of the grid.
- For each risk listed on the flip chart, ask participants to identify how likely it is that that risk will occur.
- Once you've rated the probability of each risk, start over at the top of the risk list and rate the likely impact of each risk.*

  If group members disagree, draw two 1 - 5 scales under the name of each risk and invite members to individually rank each factor, then average the scores for both Probability and Impact.

- Hand out sticky pads and assign participants the task of writing the risks on the notes. Each risk needs to be on a separate note. Invite participants to post each note on the chart based on how it was rated by the group.

- Review the final chart. Check in with each person to ensure that they can live with how the risks have been sorted.

- Divide the participants into groups of two or three.

Contingency Planning (30 minutes)	Assign each sub-group one of the issues. Start with the high impact/high probability risks. Allow at least ten minutes for each pair to discuss strategies for dealing with that risk.

- Pull the group together to hear their plans and allow everyone to add their thoughts to each set of strategies.
- Record the key points about each strategy on a flip chart.
- If time allows, repeat the process to deal with another set of risks. The risks in the low probability/low impact quadrant are typically skipped.

Next Steps (10 minutes)	

- Review and ratify strategies.
- Inform participants when and how they will receive a final contingency planning document.

Adjourn

If this is a virtual conversation:

- o Send out an email describing the need for the conversation. Ask team members to suggest who needs to be involved.
- o Distribute the seven questions on page 87 in advance of the virtual meeting. Allow at least a week for people to respond. Ask people to send you their answers. Tabulate the comments to create a single list of risks.
- o Create a survey that asks each person to rate the level of impact and the probability of each factor. Use a 1-5 scale for each indicator. Allow a week for the respondents to complete the survey. Use survey software to tabulate the results.
- o Place the risks on the Probability/Impact Grid as per the survey results. Share the completed grid.
- o Hold a videoconference or group call to discuss the results and ask for volunteers to take on the task of developing contingency plans for specific risks.
- o During this call, discuss as many of the high impact items as time allows. Ask the volunteers to take notes.
- o Set a time when all contingency plans need to be sent to you.
- o When the plans have been compiled into a final document, review them at a future virtual meeting so everyone is aware of all of the strategies.
- o Adjourn.

Structured Conversation # 7 - Stakeholder Analysis

Specifications: In every consulting assignment, some individuals are simply more important than others. These are the people who need to be constantly updated and whose needs should be in the forefront of everybody's mind. This is a conversation that you need to have early in your project - certainly before you create your general communication plan.

Since the nature of this conversation tends to be confidential, this is probably a meeting for the insiders on the project team. The timeframes shown are for a small group of from four to six participants. If you feel that you don't want to have this conversation with a group, you can nonetheless use the questions and the grid on your own to help you develop your strategy for managing stakeholders.

Purpose: To identify key stakeholders and create strategies for
effectively managing those relationships.

Agenda	Process Design Notes
Welcome (2 minutes)	• Describe the purpose of the meeting. • Review the meeting agenda. • Review and ratify the norms for the meeting. (pg. 68).
Identify Stakeholders (10 minutes)	• Facilitate a discussion to generate a list of all of the stakeholders related to the project. These can be both inside and outside the client organization. • Write all of the names on a flip chart or whiteboard. • Ask group members to also write the names on sticky notes.
Sort Stakeholders (25 minutes)	• Draw the Power/Interest Grid on a flip chart. This helps you identify who is most interested in the project, as well as who has the most power to impact the outcome.

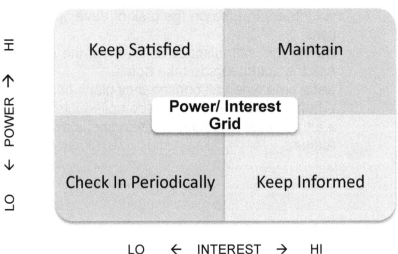

- Facilitate a discussion to sort stakeholders into the four quadrants of the grid. Be prepared for lively debate as people may not readily agree.

  - Hi Power/ Hi Interest = Maintain close contact.
  - Hi Power/Lo Interest = Keep satisfied.
  - Hi Interest/Lo Power = Keep informed.
  - Lo Interest/Lo Power = Check in periodically.

- Review the completed grid. Check with each person to ensure that they can live with how the stakeholders have been sorted.

Stakeholder Needs and Interests (30 minutes)

- Hand out a sheet with the questions listed below.

- For each stakeholder identify:

  - What are their financial and/or emotional interests?
  - What motivates them most?
  - What information do they likely want?
  - How do they want that information?

- Facilitate a discussion to build a profile of each stakeholder. Start with the high power/high interest individuals. Record comments on a flip chart to build each profile.
- When the profiles are complete, identify who needs to maintain contact with each stakeholder.

Next Steps (10 minutes)

- Decide on how you want to share the notes for the session.
- Agree on how you will update each other on these strategies as the project unfolds.

Adjourn

If this is a virtual conversation:

- o Invite project team members to send you their list of stakeholders.
- o Tabulate that input into a single list.
- o Preliminarily, sort the stakeholders using the Power/Interest Grid.
- o Share the draft grid with the team.
- o Hold a videoconference or group call to ratify the grid.
- o Decide who should manage which stakeholders.
- o Discuss the answers to the above listed questions for each of the top stakeholders.
- o Identify how you will monitor and report during the project.
- o Adjourn.

Structured Conversation # 8 - Communication Planning

Specifications: One of the challenges all outside consultants face is that they don't understand the internal communication patterns of the client organization. This structured conversation engages people inside the organization in helping to create a coherent communication plan for the project.

This meeting may need to be repeated a number of times, especially for lengthy contracts, since the players can change. In addition to this structured dialogue, remember that it's important to discuss who needs to know what at the end of every significant decision-making session.

Unlike the previous conversation that related only to key stakeholders, communication planning is about how to update employees, members of the community, suppliers, key customers and others about the progress being made. This conversation is for a small group of from four to six participants.

Purpose: To develop a communication plan for the project.

Agenda	Process Design Notes
Welcome (5 minutes)	• Describe the purpose of the meeting. • Review the meeting agenda. • Review and ratify the norms for the meeting. (pg. 68)
Identify Who (20 minutes)	• Facilitate a discussion to list the key stakeholders who need to be kept informed of developments. Record these names on the left-hand side of the flip chart.
Identify What (15 minutes)	• Ask team members to identify what each person or group needs to know.
Identify How (15 minutes)	• Ask team members to identify the form that the communications need to take: meetings, emails, conference calls, reports and presentations.
Next Steps (6 minutes)	• Review and ratify the communication plan. • Inform members when and how they will receive a typed copy of the notes from this meeting.
Adjourn	

If this is a virtual conversation:

- o Send out an email explaining the need to develop a comprehensive communication plan. Ask each person to send you a list of who needs to be kept informed about progress on the project. Tabulate that list.
- o Conduct a videoconference or phone call to share the list of stakeholders. For each person or group, identify what they need to know and how to best deliver that information.
- o Summarize this information and share it within the group.
- o Adjourn.

Structured Conversation # 9 – Status Update Meeting

Specifications: Of all the meetings you will conduct during the life of any project, the Status Update Meeting is the one that happens most often. These meetings happen anywhere from once a month to several times a week.

Status Update Meetings are about exchanging information - just presentations and current project status. They're designed to make sure that everyone's in the loop. They're not designed to generate a lot of discussion. That's what helps keep them short and to the point. This parameter needs to be stated clearly at the beginning of each of these meetings so that everyone understands the scope.

Issues or differing points of view should be noted and parked for later discussion at a well-structured decision-making meeting like the *Systematic Problem-Solving* meeting and others described in this section of the book.

While *Status Update Meeting* formats vary, most include the standard set of items described below. Note that while status update meetings are typically attended by only project team members, outsiders may be invited if there is a need to update them about the project. The typical update meeting that's attended only by project team members has from four to ten participants.

Purpose: To review progress, identify what's next, surface issues and ensure that everyone on the team is well informed.

Agenda	Process Design Notes
Welcome (5 minutes)	• Describe the purpose of the meeting. • Review the meeting agenda. • Review and ratify the norms for the meeting. (pg. 68)
Roll Call (3 minutes)	• If outsiders have been invited to the meeting, invite everyone to state their name, area of specialty and role in the project.
Accomplishments (20 minutes)	• Invite each person to briefly describe recently completed work and successes. Congratulate people on their good work. • Record these on a flip chart or whiteboard.
Status of Work (20 minutes)	• Go around the group to hear updates on progress compared to what was originally planned. Discuss both unexpected wins and the issues that others need to be aware of. • Record these on a flip chart.

Work Scheduled But Not Completed (20 minutes)	• Review any items on the work plan that were scheduled to be completed but have not been started or are behind schedule. • For each delayed item, explore the reasons for the delay and commit to a new target date. • Record these items on a flip chart.
Project Issues (5 minutes)	• Identify any ongoing issues that could affect progress and have not been resolved. • Identify who needs to work on specific issues. Set a date and time for those affected to meet to engage in a structured session of *Systematic Problem Solving* (Conversation # 12).
Imminent Actions (5 minutes)	• Ask each team member to offer a quick snapshot of what they're doing next and anything they need from other members of the team to support their actions.
Adjourn	

If this is a virtual conversation:

- o Start the videoconference or group call with a roll call.
- o Ask each person to briefly describe recently completed work and successes. Congratulate people on their good work.
- o Go around the group to hear updates on progress compared to what was originally planned. Discuss both unexpected wins and issues that others need to be aware of.
- o Review any items on the work plan that were scheduled to be completed but have not been started or are behind schedule.
- o For each delayed item, explore the reasons for the delay and commit to a new target date.
- o Identify any ongoing issues that could affect progress and that have not been resolved.
- o Identify who needs to work on specific issues. Set a date and time for those affected to meet to engage in a structured session of *Systematic Problem Solving* (Conversation # 12).
- o Ask each team member to offer a quick snapshot of what they're doing next and anything they need from other members of the team to support their actions.
- o Adjourn.

Structured Conversation # 10 – Creative Thinking

Specifications: There are times when it's important to be able to help a group think outside the box. This may be to identify a new way to deliver a service or ways to create a new product. In the past, it was common to think that only a few people in any organization were creative. To correct that mistaken assumption, the first step in running a creative thinking session is to bring together the types of people who aren't typically seen to be part of the creative process. A broad mix of participants, ranging from end-users to front-line production workers and customers, will help ward off conventional thinking.

To set the stage for this meeting, ask participants to do some homework to find at least one innovative or creative product or service. Ask them to bring in pictures or samples of these items if possible. Color photos stimulate the creative centers of the brain. In the case of services, you can ask meeting participants to conduct informal interviews in advance of the meeting. Suggest that they ask others about a recent experience with an outstanding service or to share what makes a particular product desirable. Another fruitful area of inquiry is to learn more about the problems that people are currently wrestling with. Some of the most innovative solutions come from the need to solve an existing problem.

Finally, give some thought to the meeting location. If possible, move it to a more inspiring spot than the usual meeting room. Find a space that takes people away from what they're used to seeing, to reinforce the notion of doing things differently. The ideal group size for this conversation is from eight to twelve.

> Purpose: To explore new ideas, put existing ideas together in new ways and make connections between seemingly unrelated areas to arrive at innovative solutions.

Agenda	Process Design Notes
Welcome (10 minutes)	• Describe the purpose of the meeting.
	• Review the meeting agenda and process you will use.
	• Ask people to suggest some rules for this special meeting. Ask questions like: *"What are the rules of the game for a meeting in which we truly think outside the box? What makes it possible for people to feel comfortable suggesting new things? What sorts of things should we avoid saying since they tend to put a damper on creativity?"*
	• Facilitate the development of these guidelines and record them on a flip chart.
Show and Tell (25 minutes)	• Hand out brightly colored paper and ask everyone to make notes about intriguing ideas they hear during presentations.
	• Invite each participant to talk about the examples that they

researched. If they brought pictures, post them on the wall.

- At the end of each presentation, ask the whole group to identify what makes that product or service innovative.
- Record these traits on a flip chart. If subsequent presenters mention the same trait, place a check mark beside that item. This will create a snapshot of which traits are mentioned most often.

Multi-Hat Thinking (10 minutes)

- Give each person five to ten index cards.
- Allow quiet time for each person to individually write down ideas that will improve or enhance the product or service being discussed. Suggest that they write one idea per card.
- Post a list of roles on the wall and challenge people to think like all or some of these people as they write down their ideas.
- Some suggestions for roles: Think like an eight-year-old girl, a nerdy teenage boy, an elderly person, a recent immigrant, your fiercest competitor, your best customer, a Japanese businessman, a German engineer, Steve Jobs, Elon Musk, etc.
- When each person is done, collect and shuffle the cards.
- Randomly distribute the idea cards.
- Provide the following instructions:

  - Read all of the cards that you received.
  - Keep the ones you think have real value or potential.
  - Pass the rest around the table.
  - Accumulate all the cards that add to your thinking.

Idea Blitz (25 minutes)

- Invite each person to describe the idea or ideas that they collected.
- Do not record these. Instead, quickly go around the table to hear all ideas.
- Facilitate a discussion about which concepts struck a chord. Which ones shared the same themes? Which ones belong together?

Innovation Teams (30 minutes)

- Identify patterns or ideas that belong together. Post new sheets of flip-chart paper around the room. On these flip-chart sheets, record the main ideas that belong together and the names of the people who should continue to advance that set of concepts.

Closing Comments (10 minutes)

- Allow time for the subgroups to meet to refine their thinking.
- Ask each group to create an action plan to further develop their ideas.

- Ask each person to give a brief report of the ideas they will be pursuing and their next steps.
- Invite each person to share what they gained from this meeting.

Adjourn

If this is a virtual conversation:

- Ask team members and key stakeholders to suggest participants for this creative-thinking activity.
- Call each participant and explain the need for innovation. Describe the homework.
- Set up a page on the group site for people to post the results of their research.
- Conduct a videoconference or group call to review the highlights of the ideas that were posted.
- Invite people to identify the innovative/creative traits that were demonstrated in the examples that were collected.
- Allow a few minutes of quiet time while people write down strategies that incorporate these traits.
- Facilitate a discussion to share ideas. Record these as people talk.
- Challenge people to engage in multi-hat thinking. Record any additional ideas that surface from this process.
- Continue the conversation online by posting the innovative ideas shared at this meeting on the group site. On this page, invite people to write their names next to the ideas that they're interested in pursuing.
- Coordinate these subgroups to develop their thinking further.
- Ask these teams to report back during a future videoconference or group call.

Structured Conversation # 11 – Midpoint Check

Specifications: During any consulting assignment that lasts longer than a few months, it's important to stop and assess how things are going. This meeting is designed for the project team, although it can be repeated with the leadership of the client organization. Since it surfaces issues and seeks solutions, this conversation demonstrates your ability to face problems head on.

This *Midpoint Check* activity is divided into two sections. If time allows, combine this agenda with the one that follows on *Systematic Problem Solving*. The only caution about this conversation is that it asks people to surface issues. Be sure that you invite the right people and that you create an environment in which they can be frank. The optimal group size for this activity is eight to twelve.

Purpose: To identify what is working and what's not working.

Agenda	Process Design Notes
Welcome (5 minutes)	• Describe the purpose of the meeting. • Review the meeting agenda. • Help the group develop Safety Norms (page 49).
Personal Check-in (10 minutes)	• Invite each person present to share one thing that they're personally proud of with respect to the project thus far. This can be something that the whole team accomplished or it can be a personal contribution.
Forcefield Analysis (30 minutes)	• Set up a flip chart or whiteboard as shown below.

What's working or going well? What are we doing right?	What's not working or not going well? What are we doing wrong?

- Facilitate these discussions until both sides of the page are full. These are non-decision-making conversations to simply gather ideas. There is no need to check if everyone agrees with the points you have recorded. Ideas no one supports will be tossed out during the next step. Just be sure to keep clarifying and paraphrasing to ensure that everyone understands each idea on the page.

Multi-voting
(15 minutes)

- Once all of the points are clearly understood by the participants, give each person two strips of four peel-off dots. Ask each person to write the following numbers on both sets of dots:

- Invite people to place their dots on the flip chart or whiteboard, using one strip for each side of the chart.
- On both sides of the chart the dot marked 10 should be placed on the most significant item on that list, 7 on the second most significant, and so on.
- Tally the face values of the dots. The results will indicate which items the group sees as the most significant positives and which items most need attention.

Plenary
(15 minutes)

- Review the rankings with the group.
- Explain that the next step is to explore all of the highly ranked positives to see if these can be further leveraged and to problem solve the highly ranked negatives.

Next Steps
(5 minutes)

- If time allows, proceed directly to the problem solving steps on the next page. If time is short, schedule a separate session to problem solve the highly rated negative items.
- Inform group members when they will receive the notes from the session. Clarify who will be receiving that summary.

Adjourn

If this is a virtual conversation:

- Send out an email explaining the importance of conducting a midpoint check to catch anything that isn't working and take corrective action.
- Establish a page for this activity on the team's group site.
- Post the questions as per the face-to-face agenda. Ask people not to repeat points already posted. Set a deadline for input to this step.
- Send out an email inviting people to review the completed analysis and rate the items. Use multi-voting software to identify their top four to six items in both lists. Post the results on the site.
- Hold a videoconference or group call to review the top-rated items. Invite suggestions about how to leverage the top-rated positive factors. Discuss how to tackle the top-rated negatives. Some can simply be handled by brainstorming solutions and assigning responsibility to team members.
- Identify the top-rated issues that need to become the focus of a dedicated problem-solving discussion.
- Schedule time to deal with these. Refer to the step-by-step process for *Systematic Problem Solving* that follows in this book.
- Adjourn.

Structured Conversation # 12 – Systematic Problem Solving

Specifications: One of the most important sets of steps to understand is *Systematic Problem Solving*, which allows you to assess issues and find solutions. This agenda outlines a simplified version of that multi-step process. It walks you through the key steps of analyzing an issue, identifying potential solutions, and then collaborating on a set of action plans.

The usual steps of naming the problem and stating a goal for the problem-solving exercise have been omitted. That's because these steps represent traps. Writing a complex sentence to name the problem before all of the relevant facts have been surfaced tends to lead to naming the problem incorrectly. That's why this structured conversation starts with a thorough analysis of the problem in question. You will find that doing this step first will ensure that the group arrives at a deeper understanding of the issue than would be found by writing a goal statement without that analysis.

Likewise, this structured conversation skips the step of asking group members to set a goal for the problem-solving exercise. Setting a goal opens the door for people to state the solution they favor. Jumping to solutions before conducting a thorough analysis leads to polarized thinking. The ideal group size for this activity is eight to twelve.

Purpose: To engage key stakeholders in a discovery
conversation to build an organizational profile.

Agenda	Process Design Notes
Welcome (5 minutes)	• Describe the purpose of the meeting. • Review the meeting agenda, including the steps in the problem-solving process. • Help the group create Safety Norms (page 49).
Problem Analysis (25 minutes)	• Write the name of the problem to be addressed on the flip chart or whiteboard. • Example: *Lack of coordination between the project team and the team managing the site of the new building.* • Start the analysis step by asking people to simply tell you the story of the problem. Pretend that you've never heard of the problem and just keep asking probing questions until the group has told you everything about the current situation. Remember to keep asking, *"Why? Why? Why?"* to drill down past symptoms to uncover root causes. • Some helpful things to say:

- *Describe what's going on in step-by-step detail.*

- *"Why is this happening?"*
- *"What other problems does this cause?"*
- *"Who and what contributes to this problem?"*
- *"Why hasn't this already been solved?"*

• Summarize everything group members have said in the analysis phase. Be sure that you've captured a complete picture. Remember that this is a non-decision-making conversation, so it's not necessary that everyone agrees. Differing opinions are okay.

Brainstorming (15 minutes)

• Post the analysis sheet so that everyone can see the notes.

• Invite people to brainstorm possible solutions. This is also a non-decision-making conversation, so don't let people debate ideas. Sorting the ideas comes later. You may want to post the rules of brainstorming:

- Let ideas flow: be creative, don't judge.
- Even way out ideas are good.
- Build on the ideas of others.

• Just keep recording everything that people suggest. Once the idea flow slows down, start asking probing questions like:

- *"What if we had a magic wand?"*
- *"What if money were no object?"*
- *"What if we had total power and control?"*
- *"What's the most way-out thing we could do?"*

• Post all the brainstormed ideas where everyone can see them.

Sort Ideas (10 minutes)

• With a colored marker, draw a straight line right down the middle of the page of brainstormed ideas. The line will run right through the ideas.

• On one side of the line use the colored marker to write the word ***Effort***. On the other side write the word ***Impact***.

• Then give each person two strips with 10 peel-off dots on each strip. These dots all have the same value.

• Invite people to approach the page of brainstormed ideas to place their dots. Explain the voting procedure.

• On the ***Effort*** side of the page, place dots next to all suggestions that are relatively easy to implement.

- On the ***Impact*** side of the page, place dots next to all suggestions that will have a significant impact on fixing the problem.
- Do not let people put more than one dot on a single item.

Action Planning (40 minutes)
- Tally the votes.
- On a new sheet of flip-chart paper, write down the top-ranked ideas in both categories. Make it a priority to capture those that are both high impact and easy to do.
- Help group members discuss which ideas to pursue.
- Form small groups of two to three people to take charge of the selected topics.
- Allow each group from fifteen to twenty minutes to develop next steps.
- Reconvene the group to share their action plans.

Next Steps (5 minutes)
- Set another meeting time if the group needs to repeat the process for other problems.
- Set a time to follow up on progress with the implementation of the plans created at this meeting.

Adjourn

If this is a virtual conversation:

- Send out an email explaining the process.
- Create a page for the problem-solving activity on the group site for the project team.
- Post a one to two sentence description of the problem. Post the analysis questions suggested for the face-to-face meeting. Invite people to add their comments. You can use a fishbone diagram or affinity chart or other chart if that helps sort the ideas into coherent categories. State the timeframe for adding to the problem analysis.
- Eliminate duplicate comments and streamline the analysis input. Post the results and invite team members to brainstorm ideas. If you used a chart or graph, keep that structure so that suggestions can be recorded next to the problem analysis.
- Eliminate duplicates and streamline the suggestions. Invite people to rank the suggestions using multi-voting software. Tabulate the results into a list of the top-rated suggestions.
- Hold a videoconference or group call to review the suggestions and identify actions. Assign tasks to members of the team. Set a date to receive detailed action steps.
- Make a note to review progress on implementation at a future meeting.
- Adjourn.

Structured Conversation # 13 – Constructive Controversy

Specifications: This structured conversation is designed to exploit differing points of view to ensure that ideas are thoroughly tested before they're implemented.

Unlike most meetings where you try to avoid differences of opinion, this agenda deliberately provokes controversy in order to challenge all aspects of an idea. It's the ideal approach to take when there are two or more ideas competing for approval and the group is divided about which to pursue. This dialogue works best with six to ten participants, but more people can be included.

Purpose: To encourage differing points of view in order
to thoroughly test an idea.

Agenda	Process Design Notes
Welcome (5 minutes)	• Describe the purpose of the meeting. • Review the meeting agenda. • Help the group create Safety Norms (page 49).
Advocacy Team Prep (20 minutes)	• Write the competing ideas on separate flip-chart sheets. • Invite group members to briefly explain each of the ideas. • Divide the group to form advocacy teams around the competing ideas. Allow time for each team to discuss the positives of that course of action. Ask each team to create scenarios that describe what the selected idea would look like if implemented.
Advocacy Presentations (20 minutes)	• Allow each team to present its case to the wider group. (You could invite other stakeholders to hear these presentations.) • Listeners are encouraged to make notes, but they may not speak during presentations.
Counterpoint Prep (20 minutes)	• Teams are challenged to reverse their positions on every point of their presentations. Encourage each group to identify the points against the idea they originally advocated. This can include flaws, incorrect assumptions, unanticipated reactions, execution failures, etc. This encourages each team to deepen their understanding of their own proposal.
Counterpoint Presentations (20 minutes)	• Each team presents their newly discovered counterpoints to the wider group. Listeners are encouraged to ask probing questions to help further deepen the exploration of counterpoints.

Explore Insights (20 minutes)	• Invite people to pair up with someone from the opposing team. Allow time for the pairs to share their deepened insights about both proposals. • Pull the whole group together and record the new insights on flip charts.
Decision Point (5 minutes)	• Write the name of the two proposals on a single piece of flip-chart paper or on a whiteboard. Draw a line between the proposals. • Label the proposals A and B. • Hand out a strip of ten peel-off voting dots to each person; they should all be one color. • Ask each person to mark their dots with either an A or a B to reflect the degree to which they now favor each proposal (example: eight dots marked A and two dots marked B). This voting is confidential. When dots are marked, collect them in a box or basket. • Post the dots and tally the votes. • Announce the winner of the group ranking.
Action Planning (10 minutes)	• Identify an action plan for the selected idea or strategy. Make sure that action planning takes into account coping strategies to deal with the challenges that surfaced earlier in the meeting. • Identify next steps and how minutes will be shared.
Adjourn	

If this is a virtual conversation:

• Send out an email explaining the process.
• Create a page on the group site for the constructive controversy. Ask advocates for the conflicting positions to post all of the positives of their idea. Set a timeframe during which these notes can be reviewed.
• Invite everyone on the team to write what they think are the challenges, issues, downsides, mistaken assumptions and unintended consequences of each proposal.
• During a videoconference or group call, review both the upsides and the downsides of each proposal.
• Facilitate a discussion to draw out the insights gained through this discussion.
• Invite everyone to go to the group site after the virtual meeting to distribute ten votes between the two proposals.
• Assign teams to undertake the implementation of the selected idea. Ensure that they consider all of the downsides identified during the constructive controversy process.
• Adjourn.

Structured Conversation # 14 - Survey Feedback

Specifications: Consultants often conduct surveys. These can be about employee satisfaction, customer satisfaction or the performance of a product or service. The survey can be conducted on paper the old-fashioned way, or completed and tabulated online.

Once the results are in, you will need to do something with them. The *Survey Feedback* conversation is designed to enable a group of people to review survey results together and jointly identify strategies for dealing with the items that received low ratings.

This meeting can be conducted with a small group but is actually best with a large group of twenty or more individuals. That's because a large group size makes it possible to deal with a greater number of issues. A large group also creates more anonymity and hence safety, since it allows you to create small discussion clusters.

This meeting design is ideal for a joint meeting of the project team and members of the stakeholder group. It provides a mechanism for safely dealing with sensitive issues, since all of the conversations take place in small groups, and because the design is forward looking with its emphasis on improvement strategies.

> Purpose: To engage key stakeholders in dialogue to assess
> the results of a survey and identify improvement strategies.

Agenda	Process Design Notes
Welcome (5 minutes)	• Describe the purpose of the meeting. • Review the meeting agenda. • Review and ratify the norms for the meeting. (pg. 68)
Interpreting Ratings (60 minutes)	• Divide the members into subgroups of six members. • Ask each subgroup to appoint a facilitator. Give each group only one of the low rated items on the survey. • Groups are to work through the following questions and steps in connection with the issue they were given:

- *"Why did this item get such low ratings?"* (analyze the situation)
- *"What are some actions that could improve these ratings?"* (brainstorm solutions)
- *"Which of our solutions do we think are most promising?"* (multi-vote)

Plenary (60 minutes)	• Reconvene the whole group. Invite each sub-group to present their suggestions for improvement only. (Do not let anyone talk about the reason for the poor ratings to spare people's feelings.) • Ratify their recommendation with the whole group.
Action Planning (30 minutes)	• Have members return to their original subgroups to develop action plans for ideas approved by the large group.
Plenary (30 minutes)	• Ask subgroups to report on their specific action plans for implementing improvements. • Make sure members have a plan for monitoring, reporting and follow-up.
Adjourn	

If this is a virtual conversation:

- Send out an email explaining the process. Post the survey on the group share site. Encourage people to be candid and forthright when completing the survey so that problem areas can be identified for corrective action. Specify the timeframe for completing the survey. (People will only see their own survey.)
- Share the tabulated results. Create a summary of all the items that received favorable results. List all of the items that received the lowest scores. Create a separate sheet for each of the low rated items. For about five days, allow people to anonymously type their thoughts about why each of these items received low ratings.
- At the end of the time period for input, send out a new email asking people to read all of the accumulated comments and then identify strategies for improvement that relate to the underlying causes that have been identified. Allow five days for this segment.
- Send out an email asking people to rank the suggested improvements for each survey topic. Apply multi-voting software to tabulate the results.
- Conduct a videoconference or phone call to review the top-ranked improvement suggestions. Ask for volunteers to take responsibility for developing action plans for specific items. Set timeframes for follow-up.

Structured Conversation # 15 – Interpersonal Issue Resolution

Specifications: All relationships have the potential for strife. This is especially true in consulting assignments where the stakes are high. Issues can range from differences in work styles to a clash of personalities. Regardless of the source, differences between you and your clients need to be surfaced and resolved as quickly as possible.

It's important to note that most conflict-resolution dialogues focus on airing disputes. In other words, people revisit what went wrong. This is dangerous for a number of reasons. First, rehashing the past tends to reopen wounds. Second, it tends to feel confrontational. Little wonder that most people practice avoidance when it comes to resolving interpersonal issues.

This conversation offers a safer and more constructive approach. Instead of dredging up the past, it invites the parties in a dispute to describe exactly what they need from each other going forward. For example, instead of telling someone that they have been communicating poorly in the past, you would simply tell them that you need a simple bullet point summary of important information via email at the end of each day. The best requests are detailed, specific and avoid all judgment about the past.

This is an ideal dialogue to have at the midpoint of any project, even when there are no outward signs of trouble. Think of it as a proactive way of getting ahead of issues before they become problems. Because of the nature of this conversation, it's best reserved for small groups: you and the person who hired you; you and your inner team; you and one member of the team with whom you're experiencing friction. Even though this is a private chat, it should never be conducted over lunch or in a public place. Seek a private room to avoid disruptions. You may find it helpful to also review the steps of resolving a dispute between two parties on page 59 in the chapter on conflict management.

Purpose: To identify specific actions, two people in a dispute can
take to resolve their issues and improve the relationship.

Agenda	Process Design Notes
Welcome (3 minutes)	• Describe the purpose of the meeting. • Review the process. • Propose the rules on page 60. Ask participants to accept these. Invite them to add additional rules.

Set the Stage (2 minutes)	• State that you want to explore how you can work together even more effectively. Explain that this is a forward-looking dialogue in which you're looking for very specific things that you can do to improve your services and also how you interact with the client organization.
Invite Input (15 minutes)	• Invite the client to state what they need from you in order for you to become even more effective in working with them. • Offer an example: *"For example, if you think that I don't communicate often enough, tell me exactly when and how you want me to communicate. You don't need to tell me what's gone wrong in the past, just what I can do to improve things. I'm looking for about four or five really specific things that I can implement immediately to improve how we work together."* • Listen actively, ask probing questions and paraphrase the key points that the other person makes. Stay completely neutral and do not refute any requests at this stage. Calmly accept all suggestions, even if you don't agree with them. • Make notes to demonstrate that you're really hearing their input. When the other person is done, read your notes back to make sure that you've accurately understood the expressed needs.
Make Offers (5 minutes)	• Respond to the needs that have been expressed by making very specific offers. For example, if the other party stated a need for a daily bullet point update, say that you will provide that update and the time of day when the person can expect to receive it. • *(Note that some of the things expressed may actually be problems that need to be solved in a separate problem-solving meeting using the structured dialogue outlined on page 101.)* • If the other party seems satisfied with the offers that you've made, move along to the next phase of the conversation.
Offer Input (15 minutes)	• Ask the other party if you can express your needs. Explain that in some instances, you may not be able to respond to their needs unless you've received specific support from them. • State what you need from the other person in clear

and non-emotional language. Avoid going into the past to give examples of how things went wrong. This can lead you into the dangerous territory of rehashing the past. Stick to what you need going forward. For example you might say: *"I need to receive all minutes from the senior management meeting that impact my project as soon as those meetings are over."*

- Share any other needs that you have.

Request Offers (10 minutes)

- Review the list of your needs when you're done and ask the other person to suggest what they could do in response.

Closure (5 minutes)

- Summarize the other person's offers.
- Commit to writing up the two lists of offers. Specify when it will be shared.
- Thank the other person for taking the time to discuss how the relationship can be improved.

Adjourn

If this is a virtual conversation:

- Make a personal phone call to the other person to express your desire to explore ways of further improving the relationship.
- Explain that you want to schedule a personal phone call to discuss specific things that that person would like you to do in order to improve project management.
- Explain that you will make specific offers back to that person once you have seen their list of needs. Offer a couple of examples. Offer to allow the other party to send you their list of needs via email if that's easier for them.
- Set a time to talk about their needs and to make offers.
- Gain their approval to make the process work in both directions.
- Share your list of needs. Accept offers made by the client.
- Indicate when you will share both offers lists.

Structured Conversation # 16 – Overcoming Resistance

Specifications: It's very common for people to resist change. The standard approach to getting through resistance is to communicate a compelling vision to get people inspired. This is nothing more than glorified selling. It not only doesn't work, but will likely drive the resistance underground. In other words, people may pretend that they approve of the changes, but passively resist implementation.

Facilitators take a very different approach to managing resistance: they engage people in honest dialogue about why they're stuck, and then support them while they identify what they need to be able to move forward.

If your project encounters resistance and you want to really find out why people are pushing back, consider having a conversation based on the following agenda. It works with a small group, but is actually more effective if you can get more than twenty people to take part. The larger group size provides greater anonymity and yields more recommendations. Refer to page 58 for more about the principles of dealing with resistance.

Purpose: To identify resistance to change and
develop strategies to move forward.

Agenda	Process Design Notes
Welcome (5 minutes)	• Describe the purpose of the meeting. • Review the meeting agenda.
Set the Stage (15 minutes)	• Openly state that it's normal for people to resist change. Make an optimistic statement that you want to explore the reasons for the resistance in a forward-looking conversation. • Help the group create a special set of norms for this meeting. • Post a starter set of norms on a flip-chart sheet. Ask everyone to find a partner to identify additional rules that will make everyone feel that they can participate freely in the discussion. Refer to the Safety Norms on page 49 for that starter set. • Hold a quick plenary to gather up the suggestions of additional norms from the partners. Write them up, then ratify them with the whole group to ensure that everyone can live with them.

Introduce the
Resistance
Model
(5 minutes)

- Post a sketch of the four-stage resistance model that's shown below.
- Explain that the people impacted by change react to it in the following four ways. Identifying exactly what people are resisting and at what level, opens the door to finding solutions that help unblock resistance to change.

Commitment – Bought In. "Let's go!!"
Exploration – Open. "I'm willing to try."
Resistance – Actively work against change. "I will not help with change."
Denial – Ignore change. "It will go away."

Identifying
What and Why
(40 minutes)

- Divide participants into four small groups. Move the groups into four corners of the room. Give each group a flip chart and ask them to appoint someone to take notes.
- Assign each group one of the four stages in the resistance model and challenge them to answer the following questions as they relate to that category.*

  - Which aspects of the change are being resisted at this level?
  - Who is resisting the changes?
  - Why is the resistance happening?
  - How can we move people forward?

- Allow groups ten minutes for discussion and to record their responses. (*Note that the commitment group will be looking at why people are bought-in and how that commitment can be leveraged.)
- Stop the action.
- Ask each group to get up and move around the room to the next flip chart. Ask the recorders to stay put so

that they can read to the next group what has already been discussed. Allow five minutes for the new group to add their thoughts.
- Stop the action.
- After five minutes, move the groups again.
- Stop the action.
- After five more minutes, move the groups one last time.
- Stop the action when everyone has visited each topic.

Identifying How (40 minutes)	<ul><li>Now that each person has taken part in all four conversations, have them return to the flip chart where they started. The recorder will read them the suggestions made by the whole group for that resistance category.</li><li>Have group members assess and ratify the suggested strategies to overcome resistance or leverage commitment.</li><li>Ask each recorder to read out the strategies ratified by the groups. Invite comments from the large group.</li></ul>
Sort Ideas (5 minutes)	<ul><li>Hand out strips of stick-on voting dots or give each person a colored marker.</li><li>Invite everyone to walk past all four flip charts so that they can identify the two or three ideas on each flip chart that should be implemented.</li><li>Tally the votes.</li></ul>
Action Planning (60 minutes)	<ul><li>Record the top-ranked strategies for overcoming resistance or leveraging commitment on a flip chart at the front of the room.</li><li>Ask small groups of two to three people to volunteer to head up action teams to plan and follow through on the top-ranked items.</li><li>If there's time, ask them to identify immediate next steps and set a schedule for further planning.</li><li>Create a mechanism to follow up on progress.</li><li>Thank everyone for their candor and participation.</li></ul>

Adjourn

If this is a virtual conversation:

- o Send out an email explaining that resistance to change is natural and that it represents an important opportunity to look for ideas to move things forward. Set a timeframe for gathering input.
- o Create a page on the team's group site for this activity. Include an illustration of the four stages of resistance model described earlier. Include

instructions that you're looking for very specific examples of resistance: who is resisting which changes and why. Offer at least one example to show the level of detail you're looking for. Also invite people to offer examples of high buy-in for the commitment category.

o Hold a videoconference or conference call to review the data collected. Encourage people to discuss the data so that everyone in the group has a shared understanding of the resistance factors.

o Hold a verbal multi-vote: invite each person to identify the top three blocks that need to be addressed. This will surface a list of the key blocks. Do the same for the items in the commitment box.

o Facilitate brainstorming to generate strategies for addressing each resistance factor and for leveraging existing buy-in.

o Summarize and ratify the strategies the group feels are worth pursuing and assign people to develop action plans. Identify the next step for implementing actions and reporting on results.

o Adjourn.

Structured Conversation # 17 - Project Retrospective

Specifications: At the end of a project, it's important to identify lessons learned. To get a wide range of perspectives, a group of between fifteen and thirty participants is recommended. The large group lets you create small subgroups. This provides more anonymity and hence yields a more honest assessment.

Before the meeting, you will need to create a large chart that displays a detailed, top-down flow chart of the project. This chart should show the stages and timeline of the entire project. Post this chart in the meeting room. Distribute a small version of this project map to the participants in advance of the session so that they can refresh their memories. Note that since any retrospective involves some level of critique, it's important to engage people in setting rules or norms of conduct so that people feel comfortable surfacing problems.

Purpose: To debrief the project to identify what worked
and to glean lessons learned.

Agenda	Process Design Notes
Welcome (5 minutes)	• Describe the purpose of the meeting. • Review the meeting agenda. • Ask members to suggest rules or norms that will make everyone feel that they can be totally candid about the project. Consider using the Safety Norms on page 49 as a starter set.
Positive Elements (25 minutes)	• Give each person a sticky note pad and allow time for them to write down all the positive events that took place during the project. This could be things that were done well, achievements, breakthroughs, good teamwork, etc. • Invite everyone to approach the map and post their notes on the map at the point when these events occurred. People can read these out as they are posting them. • Facilitate a large group discussion about the strengths of the project: what went well, when these things happened and who added to the successful aspects. Record the positives on a flip chart. • Hand out strips of sticky dots that are weighted. Invite attendees to come up and rank the positive elements. • Tally the votes and review the scores.
Pitfalls (10 min)	• Give each person a sticky note pad of a different color. Allow time for people to write down all the negative events that took place during the project.

115

This could be things that were done poorly, mistakes, mishaps, lack of teamwork, conflict, etc.
- Invite people to approach the map and post their notes on the map at the point where each of these events occurred. These should not be read out.
- Allow group members to read all of the notes by milling around.

Lessons Learned (20 Minutes)
- Invite people to sort themselves into subgroups, with one small group for each project stage.
- Give each group the sticky notes for the project stage that they're assessing.
- Allow at least twenty minutes for the groups to discuss the issues on their sticky notes. Have them: 1) analyze each issue as to what went wrong and why, and 2) identify lessons learned and what could be done in future to avoid a repeat of each mistake or mishap.

Plenary (15 minutes)
- Reconvene the group. Ask each group to share lessons learned and future recommendations. Do not rehash the past.
- Record suggestions at the front of the room. Invite questions and comments.
- Thank everyone for taking part.

Adjourn

If this is a virtual conversation:

- o Create an intranet page displaying the top-down project map. Add a brief description of what was accomplished at each stage.
- o Send out an email inviting people to visit the page to identify what worked well and also what did not work well at each stage. Set a specific timeframe to gather this data. Point out that all comments are anonymous.
- o Invite participants to review each other's comments. Provide a mechanism for rating both the positive and the negative assessments.
- o Use multi-voting software to rank both sets of comments. Tabulate the results and share the assessment.
- o Hold a videoconference or group call to identify lessons learned and recommendations about how to avoid the top-ranked issues or mishaps.
- o Describe how the information from this process will be shared.
- o Adjourn.

Structured Conversation # 18 – Project Adjournment

Specifications: The completion of a project represents an opportunity to end on a positive note. This conversation is somewhat intimate, so it works best with a small group of from six to ten people. Whether you use all of the steps as outlined below, or create a less formal version, this conversation is a reminder about how important it is to celebrate success with the people who made it happen.

Note that if you're uncomfortable with the personal nature of this discussion, this activity can be conducted virtually. Just set up a feedback page, then send each team member an invitation to make a positive comment under the photo of the other team members. It needs to be said, however, that nothing beats the positive impact of having this discussion in person.

Purpose: To end a consulting assignment on a positive note.

Agenda	Process Design Notes
Welcome (5 minutes)	• Describe the purpose of the meeting. • Explain the meeting agenda.
Strength Bombardment (25 minutes)	• Give each person a blank sheet of paper. Ask them to write their name on the top of the sheet and pass the blank sheet to the person on their left. • Allow quiet time while each person writes a positive comment on the sheet they have just been handed. This can be a personal trait, something that person did that was appreciated, etc. Ask people to keep passing the sheets until everyone has written at least one comment on each person's page.
Strength Sharing (10 minutes)	• When everyone has their personal feedback sheet in front of them, start the sharing. • Ask someone to begin. That person will pass his completed sheet to the person to his left. Person No. 2 reads aloud what she wrote on that sheet. This sheet is then passed to Person No. 3 who reads aloud what he wrote to Person No. 1. That same sheet continues to be passed around the group until each person has read out what they wrote to Person No. 1. When the first person's sheet comes back to them, repeat for Person No. 2. Continue until everyone has had the positive comments on their sheet read aloud in front of the whole group.

| Closing
(2 minutes) | • Invite each person to describe the most valuable thing they've gained from the feedback.
• Share your personal takeaway.

• Thank everyone for taking part in the exercise and for everything that they contributed to the success of the project.
• Thank the client for the opportunity of assisting them in their pursuit of excellence. |

Adjourn

If this is a virtual conversation:

○ Create a team page on the group site. Post each person's picture.
○ Send out an email that invites everyone on the team to go to the site to add a positive comment under each team member's photo. This can include positive personal traits, how they went above and beyond, or what was most appreciated. Set a timeframe for the posting of comments.
○ Hold a videoconference or group call to review the positive feedback. Ask people to read out the feedback that was sent to other teammates.
○ Invite each person to share what they're personally taking away from the project. Share your own takeaway.
○ Thank everyone for their contribution to the success of the project.
○ Adjourn.

Enhance Your Facilitation Skills

The best way to improve your skills in front of groups is to take a Facilitation Skills Workshop. If you have the time and money, consider attending a facilitation skills workshop that features practice rounds and observer feedback. Providers vary by geography, but can easily be found by conducting an online search for either *Facilitator Training* or *Facilitation Skills Workshops.* This is absolutely the best way to accelerate your learning curve.

Enroll in an Online Facilitation Skills Course

If you can't spare the time to attend a workshop, there is an online option available through our website. This is the only online course on the subject of facilitation skills in existence. This course isn't the usual boring set of slides you get with most online courses. Our program features forty-seven video clips showing both the right and the wrong way to facilitate. There's a test at the end of the course which results in a certificate of completion. The cost for six months of unlimited access is $99.00 for a single enrollment, with discounts for groups going as low as $15.00 per person.

View program details on the next page

View the program outline on the next page.
Preview a lesson on our website.
www.facilitationtutor.com
Send an email to obtain a free preview enrollment.
Ingrid@facilitationtutor.com

The Facilitation Skills Online Program   (3 to 5 hours viewing time)

- The program is organized into ten lessons.
- Each lesson isolates a single, important technique.
- Each core skill is demonstrated in a group setting.
- Theoretical models are clearly and simply explained.
- Interactive exercises and structured practice activities accompany each lesson.
- Each lesson is supported by downloadable workbook pages.
- The program is linked to an online bookstore, featuring recommended further reading.
- A final test allows learners to receive a Certificate of Completion.

Lesson 1 – Introduction to Facilitation

- introduces the concept of facilitation: its purpose and underlying beliefs
- provides an overview of the foundational content/process model
- clarifies misunderstanding about facilitator assertiveness
- examines how leaders can balance facilitating with being directive.

Lesson 2 – The Five Core Practices

- describes the five core practices of facilitation
- demonstrates the five core practices in action
- explores the boundaries of neutrality
- recommends ways to use the five core practices in various settings.

Lesson 3 – The Start Sequence

- provides a clear structure for beginning any facilitated session
- offers examples of start sequences of varying complexity
- shows how the start sequence can be used to maintain focus throughout any facilitated session.

Lesson 4 – Establishing Norms

- explores the challenging situations that occur in meetings
- shows how *Norming* can create and maintain a positive meeting climate
- demonstrates how targeted *Norming* can be used to deal with difficult situations.

Lesson 5 – Recording Group Ideas

- describes the purpose and importance of flip-chart note taking
- creates awareness of both the best and worst practices of recording group ideas
- describes the rules of wording and demonstrates them in action.

Lesson 6 – Conflict Intervention Techniques

- emphasizes the importance of assertively managing conflict in groups
- provides a technique for intervening to redirect member behaviors
- shares a specific model for addressing group conflict that is both non-confrontational and effective
- provides guidance for getting through those difficult moments in any meeting.

Lesson 7 – Process Checking

- explores the hidden reasons that meetings falter
- provides a specific set of steps for taking the pulse and restoring group effectiveness
- shares techniques for conducting written process checks.

Lesson 8 – Conversation Structure

- describes the two categories of conversations
- provides strategies for the two types of conversations to manage complex decision-making discussions
- offers specific strategies for managing the dynamic shift between these two modes.

Lesson 9 – Decision-Making Tools

- outlines the various ways that groups can make decisions and clarify whether they unite or divide group members
- demonstrates situations in which each approach is applicable
- illustrates how various decision-making tools can be used in combination to arrive at solutions everyone can live with.

Lesson 10 – Ending a Facilitation

- provides a checklist of what facilitators do to effectively end facilitated discussions
- demonstrates a variety of ways to bring closure
- provides tools for overcoming blocks to consensus
- provides a format for action planning
- shares strategies to avoid poor follow-through.

Prices for the online course range from $99.00 for a single enrollment to $15.00 for a group of over 500 participants.

If you have questions about the online program, send an email to:

Ingrid@facilitationtutor.com

Facilitator Certification

Certified Professional Facilitator

The top designation in the field is granted by the *International Association of Facilitators (IAF)*. This body conducts a review process that leads to the designation of *Certified Professional Facilitator (CPF)*.

The *CPF* process consists of the following steps: Applicants must have at least ten years experience as a group facilitator. Each applicant is asked to submit a paper describing six recent facilitation activities that they designed and led. Each facilitation case study cited must be accompanied by a signed letter from each of the clients mentioned. The applicant then attends a two-day assessment meeting in one of the cities posted on the *IAF* website. Locations change every six months or so. At the event, each applicant facilitates a complex discussion with a group of their fellow applicants while a review panel observes. After a lengthy debriefing session, the panel decides whether or not to grant the *Certified Professional Facilitator* designation. The fee for taking part is approximately $1,500.00, plus the cost of travel and accommodation. To learn more about the *CPF* process go to www.iafworld.org.

Validated Facilitator Certification

Since the *CPF* process described above is accessible only to those who have been in practice for at least ten years, a more accessible certification process was created by *The Pfeiffer Company*, a leader in the development of tests and instruments. In 2009, they asked Ingrid Bens, the author of this book and the international best seller *Facilitating with Ease!*, to create a reliable test to assess facilitator competency. The result was the *Facilitation Skills Inventory (FSI)*.

The *FSI* is a test of twenty observable skills that must be mastered by all facilitators. To be assessed, all you need to do is find a facilitator colleague who is willing to observe you in action during a group meeting of at least one hour's length. After the meeting, the observer completes the inventory and offers specific feedback during a post-observation coaching session.

The *FSI* criteria yields results that show a facilitator to be at one of three levels: Developing, Accomplished or Advanced. Because the *FSI* test was developed over three years with rigorous validation by a panel of certified professionals, these test results can be cited in resumes.

The Facilitation Skills Inventory is readily available on Amazon. If you want to be able to add a validated facilitation certification level to your next resume, simply purchase two of the FSI booklets: the *Participant Guide* and the *Observer Guide*, then find someone to observe and rate your performance. These cost approximately $25.00 each. You can also buy the instrument at www.wiley.com.

Author Biography

Ingrid Bens is the President of Facilitation Tutor, which is a consulting firm created to further the practice of facilitation as a core leadership competency. Ingrid has a Master's Degree in Adult Education and over 25 years of experience as an Organization Development consultant.

Her consulting experience includes the design and facilitation of numerous large-scale, strategic change efforts in a number of Fortune 500 companies, government agencies and nonprofit organizations. Ingrid has consulted on numerous team implementation projects in banks, hospitals, research firms, educational institutions and manufacturing plants. She has led many projects to improve employee morale and help management shift to a more inclusive approach to leadership.

Ingrid Bens is the well-known author of multiple bestselling books on the topic of facilitation, most notably *Facilitating with Ease!,* which is in its third edition and which has been translated into multiple languages, including Chinese. She is also the author of *Advanced Facilitation Strategies and Facilitating to Lead,* plus the Memory Joggers entitled *Facilitation at a Glance!* and *The Conflict Handbook.* In 2009 Ingrid Bens was asked by Pfeiffer Publishing to create the *Facilitation Skills Inventory* (*FSI*). This is currently the only validated instrument available for the assessment of facilitator competency.

When she isn't consulting or writing, Ingrid Bens conducts workplace seminars on facilitation skills, team management and conflict skills. She has taught workshops across the United States, as well as in Canada, Europe and Asia. Her extensive client list includes General Electric, Honeywell, The International Monetary Fund, Merck, CitiGroup, The Department of Veteran's Affairs, McCormick Foods, Hess Oil, Gannett Publishing, Keurig Green Mountain, The Banff Center for Management, The National Education Association, The Environmental Protection Agency, A.A.R.P., Alcon, The Federal Deposit Insurance Commission, The National Institute for School Leadership, Harley-Davidson, Boeing, KPMG Consulting, The Securities Exchange Commission, NASA, Philadelphia Children's Hospital, the National Oceanographic and Atmospheric Administration, Genzyme and US Bank.

Chapter References

Axelrod, R. *The Evolution of Cooperation.* New York: Basic Books, 1984.

Beckhard, R. *Organization Development: Strategies and Models.* Reading, MA: Addison-Wesley, 1969.

Beckhard, R., & Harris, R. *Organizational Transitions: Managing Complex Change.* 2nd ed., Boston: Addison-Wesley, 1987.

Bens, I. *Facilitating With Ease!* (3rd ed.). San Francisco. Jossey-Bass. 2012.

Bracken, D. W., Timmreck, C. W., & Church, A. H., eds. *The Handbook of Multi-Source Feedback.* San Francisco: Jossey-Bass, 2001.

Bradford, L. P., ed. *Group Development.* San Diego: University Associates, 1978.

Brown, S., & Fisher, R. *Getting Together.* New York: Penguin Publishing, 1992.

Dotlich, D., & Cairo, P. *Action Coaching.* San Francisco: Jossey-Bass, 1999.

Duarte, D. L., & Snyder, N. T., *Mastering Virtual Teams,* 2nd ed.. San Francisco: Jossey-Bass, 2001.

Fairhurst, G., & Sarr, R. *The Art of Framing.* San Francisco: Jossey-Bass, 1996.

Fink, A. *The Survey Handbook.* Thousand Oaks, CA: Sage Publishing, 1995.

Forsyth, D. R. *Group Dynamics.* Pacific Cove, CA: Brooks/Cole, 1990.

French, W., & Bell, C., Jr. *Organization Development: Behavioral Science Interventions for Organization Improvement.* 3rd ed., Englewood Cliffs, NJ: Prentice-Hall, 1990.

Fisher, A. B. *Small Group Decision Making: Communication and Group Process.* New York: McGraw-Hill, 1974.

Harrison, R. "Choosing the Depth of Organizational Intervention." *The Journal of Applied Behavioral Science* l of. 6 (2), 181-202, 1970.

Hart, L. B. *Faultless Facilitation.* Amherst, MA: H.R.D. Press, 1992.

Heron, J. *Group Facilitation: Theories and Models for Practice.* London, UK; Kogan Page, 1993.

Hersey, P. & Blanchard, K. *Management of Organizational Behavior: Utilizing Human Resources.* (4th ed.). Englewood Cliffs, NJ: Prentice Hall, 1982.

Higgs, A. C., & Ashworth, S. D. *Organizational Surveys: Tools for Assessment and Change.* San Francisco: Jossey-Bass, 1996.

Howell, J. L. *Tools for Facilitating Team Meetings.* Seattle: Integrity Publishing,1995.

Kaner, S. *Facilitator's Guide to Participatory Decision-Making.* Philadelphia: New Society Publishers, 1996.

Kaufman, R. *Identifying and Solving Problems.* San Diego: University Associates, 1976.

Kayser, T. A. *Mining Group Gold.* Sequido, CA: Serif Publishing, 1990.

Keating, C. J. *Dealing With Difficult People.* New York: Paulist Press, 1984.

Kindler, H. S. *Managing Disagreement Constructively.* Los Altos, CA: Crisp Publications, 1988.

Likert, R., & Likert, J. G. *New Ways of Managing Conflict.* New York: McGraw-Hill,1976.

Levine S. *Getting Resolution: Turning Conflict Into Collaboration.* San Francisco: Berrett-Koehler, 1999.

Locke, E., & Latham, G. *Goal Setting.* Englewood Cliffs, NJ: Prentice Hall, 1984.

McPherson, J. H. *The People, the Problems and the Problem-Solving Methods.* Midland, MI: The Pendell Company,1967.

Means, J., & Adams, T. *Facilitating the Project Lifecycle.* San Francisco. Jossey-Bass, 2005.

Means, J., Adams, T., & Spivey, M. *The Project Meeting Facilitator.* San Francisco. Jossey-Bass, 2007.

Mindell, P. *How to Say IT for Executives.* New York: Prentice Hall Press, 2005.

Mosvick, R., & Nelson, R. *We've Got to Start Meeting Like This!* New York: Scott, Foresman and Company, 1987.

Nadler, D. A. *Feedback and Organization Development: Using Data-Based Methods.* Reading, MA: Addison-Wesley,1977.

Nelson, B. *1001 Ways to Energize Employees.* New York: Workman Publishing, 1997.

Pfeiffer, J. W., & Jones, J. E. *A Handbook of Structured Experiences for Human Relations Training* (vols 1 -X). San Francisco, CA, 1972.

Reddy, B. *Intervention Skills: Process Consultation for Small Groups and Teams.* San Francisco: Jossey-Bass/Pfeiffer, 1994.

Rees, F. *The Facilitator Excellence Handbook.* San Francisco: Jossey-Bass/Pfeiffer, 1998.

Saint, S., & Lawson, J. R. *Rules for Reaching Consensus.* San Francisco. Jossey-Bass/Pfeiffer, 1994.

Strachen, D. *Questions That Work.* Ottawa, Canada: ST Press, 2001.

Stanfield, R. B., ed. *The Art of Focused Conversation.* Toronto, Canada: ICA Canada, 2000.

Taglere, D. A. *How to Meet, Think and Work to Consensus.* San Diego: Pfeiffer & Company, 1992.

Van Gundy, A. B. *Techniques of Structured Problem Solving.* New York: Van Nostrand Reinhold, 1981.

Vengel, A. *The Influence Edge: How to Persuade Others to Help You Achieve Your Goals.* San Francisco: Berret-Koehler, 1998.

Wheatley, M. J. *Leadership and the New Science: Learning About Organizations From an Orderly Universe.* San Francisco: Berrett-Koehler, 1992.

Wilson, P. H. *The Facilitative Way.* Shawnee Mission, KS: TeamTech Press, 2003.

Weisbord, M. R. *Organizational Diagnosis: A Workbook of Theory and Practice,* Josey-Bass. San Francisco, CA, 1991.

Wood, J. T., Phillips, G. M., & Pederson, D. J. *Group Discussion: A Practical Guide to Participation and Leadership* (2nd ed.). New York: Harper and Row, 1986.

Zander, A. *Making Groups Effective.* San Francisco: Jossey-Bass, 1983.

Buy In Quantity and Save!

If you're thinking of buying this book for a large group, contact us for a better price. We can drop ship any quantity. Group purchases start at 10 books.

1 - 9 copies	$32.00
10 – 99 copies	25% discount
100 - 249 copies	30% discount
250 - 499 copies	35% discount
500 and up	Contact us for a quote

Make It Your Own

Include your motto, mission and logo on the outside and inside covers, even add a page with your personal message. We can also create a custom front and back cover for a fee. Drop us an email at the address below to request the full details of customization.

Ingrid@facilitationtutor.com

CPSIA information can be obtained
at www.ICGtesting.com
Printed in the USA
LVHW060744140222
711073LV00007B/213